Practical Home Handbook

Embroidery

Skills & Techniques

Practical Home Handbook

Embroidery
Skills & Techniques

Dorothy Wood

LORENZ BOOKS

This edition published by
Lorenz Books in 2002

© Anness Publishing Limited 2000, 2002

Lorenz Books is an imprint of
Anness Publishing Limited
Hermes House
88–89 Blackfriars Road
London SE1 8HA

Published in the USA by
Lorenz Books
Anness Publishing Inc.
27 West 20th Street
New York, NY 10011

www.lorenzbooks.com

This edition distributed in Canada
by Raincoast Books
9050 Shaughnessy Street
Vancouver
British Columbia V6P 6E5

A CIP catalogue record for this book
is available from the British Library.

Publisher: Joanna Lorenz
Project editor: Simona Hill
Step-by-step photography:
    Rodney Forte
Special photography: Nicky Dowey
Illustrator: Penny Brown
Designer: Margaret Sadler

Previously published as *Embroidery*
and as part of a larger compendium,
The Practical Encyclopedia of Sewing

10 9 8 7 6 5 4 3 2 1

CONTENTS

INTRODUCTION

For centuries embroidery has been a satisfying and creative way to decorate clothing and to add a personal touch to items for the home, such as table linen and bed linen. Traditional hand embroidery stitches are still popular today, and this book features a comprehensive directory of stitches clearly illustrated with photographs and diagrams. This is accompanied by demonstrations of the different embroidery techniques, including shisha work, ribbon embroidery and counted-thread work, illustrated with beautiful historical examples and techniques to follow. Among the many other lovely techniques described are drawn-thread work, Hardanger and broderie anglaise, all of which are usually worked in cream or white. Beadwork, goldwork and couching evoke the richly decorated garments of medieval courtiers. Today all of these varied techniques are adapted by modern embroiderers to create original textiles that are valued as works of art in their own right.

Machine embroidery has revolutionized traditional embroidery, and many embroiderers combine both hand and machine techniques in one piece of work. A sewing machine can be used, changing the machine feet, such as the darning foot, and altering the tension to create a wide range of decorative textures and effects. Full details are given at the end of the book on how to get the most from your sewing machine.

Advice is also given on such matters as colouring the background fabric, the results obtained on different fabrics, transferring a design, and how to use an embroidery hoop or frame. Water-soluble fabric is an exciting development that allows you to create three-dimensional, sculptural shapes, taking the traditional craft of embroidery into a new era in the twenty-first century.

Materials and equipment

For those new to hand embroidery, one of the pleasures of this craft lies in the simplicity of the equipment. For little outlay, and a bit of imagination, you can decorate and embellish a wide range of furnishings and clothes. The basic equipment – needles, threads (floss) and an embroidery hoop or frame – is readily available. If your interest lies in machine embroidery, a basic zigzag sewing machine will suffice.

1 Beads

Many different sizes and shapes of bead can be used in embroidery. They can be sewn on individually or couched in rows. Seed beads can be used to add texture to canvas work, cross stitch and other flat embroidery techniques.

2 Fabrics

Fabrics as diverse as plain calico and luxurious silk dupion are suitable for embroidery. The choice depends on the finished look you want to achieve. Even very delicate fabrics can be used with a backing fabric.

Use an even-weave fabric such as canvas, linen, Hardanger or Aida for counted-thread embroidery. These techniques require fabrics that have a distinct weave, which allows you to work even, regular stitches. Freestyle embroidery and ribbonwork can be stitched on almost any ordinary fabric.

3 Hoops and frames

Hold your fabric in a frame or hoop while you are embroidering it. The most popular frame used for hand embroidery is a wooden hoop, available in a number of different sizes. A medium sized 18–20cm/ 7–8in hoop is comfortable to hold and you can move it across the fabric as the embroidery is completed.

For machine embroidery, use a wooden hoop upside down or a purpose-made plastic hoop that fits easily under the darning foot.

4 Needles

Crewel needles are the best needles to use for embroidery. They have large eyes that make threading easy and come in various sizes. Chenille needles look like crewel needles but are much larger. They can be used to take thick couched threads through to the wrong side of the fabric. Tapestry needles have a blunt point, which makes them ideal for even-weave fabrics.

For machine embroidery, use a heavier needle (80/12 or 90/14) to prevent the needle bending and breaking. For thicker, fancy threads use an embroidery needle that has a much larger eye. Each time you change the thread, change the needle.

5 Scissors

Embroidery scissors are essential for fine, hand embroidery. They have short blades for accurately cutting threads or trimming small pieces of fabric. The long, thin, pointed blades can be used to remove stitches without damaging the background fabric. Never use sewing scissors for cutting paper because this will soon blunt the blades.

6 Ribbons

Use either synthetic or silk ribbons for embroidery. They are available in a wide range of colours and in three widths, 2mm/^{1}/₁₆in, 4mm/^{3}/₁₆in and 7mm/^{5}/₁₆in, and are suitable for a wide range of different embroidery stitches.

7 Threads (floss)

You can buy some wonderful threads (floss) for hand embroidery in many different colours, textures and weights. The most popular one, stranded cotton, is a versatile thread made up of six strands of twisted cotton. It is used for cross stitch and hand embroidery. Coton à broder and soft cotton are both single-strand cotton threads. Coton perlé is a twisted round thread with a deep shine, used for canvas work and hand embroidery.

Viscose rayon threads are also becoming more popular. These are stranded threads with a silky sheen available in rich, luxurious colours. Flower or Nordin thread is a rustic single-strand thread that works very well on homespun fabrics. For really special embroidery, try using silk threads. There are a great many specialist embroidery threads, some plain and others fancy or metallic.

Machine embroidery thread is finer than sewing thread with a loose twist so that the threads will shine. Some fancy threads can be wound on to the bobbin and stitched with the fabric upside down.

Preparation for hand stitching

With beautiful threads (floss) to hand and an idea of the finished piece in your mind's eye, curb your enthusiasm to start work until your preparation is complete. Ensuring that the fabric is painted or coloured exactly as you want and is dry enough to begin, that the design has been transferred accurately, and that the fabric is held taut in a hoop or frame will ensure your progress is not hindered and that better results are achieved.

Colouring the fabric

There are many ways you can embellish fabric for embroidery, for example, by adding pieces of appliqué or by colouring it with dyes or paints before you start. The entire fabric can be dyed, using techniques such as space- or tie-dyeing. Sections of the design can be coloured using wax or gutta to restrict the flow of the dye.

You can also use temporary masking techniques, templates and masking tape to spray-paint, sponge or stencil a design on to fabric. Water-based fabric paints are available in many colours for home use. Splatters can be washed off easily and the dry paint can be set using a household iron.

Right: 1 brushes, 2 silk paints, 3 sponge, 4 fabric paints, 5 gutta, 6 oil sticks.

Resist techniques

Resist-dyeing methods such as batik, tie-dye and gutta all use the same principle to create a wide variety of effects.

Batik is a traditional dyeing technique that uses wax to resist the dye. Hot wax is applied with a brush or a tool called a "tjanting" so that after the fabric has been dyed the waxed areas remain unchanged in colour. Several colours can be added, waxing each time, to build up the design.

Tie-dye is another technique that can be used to create a wide range of patterns. Wonderful bold and delicate designs can be achieved: rolling a piece of fabric over a thick cord and tying the ends before dyeing can produce an amazing mottled snakeskin appearance. Tritik is another simple technique that creates a variety of patterns. For this, pieces of fabric are gathered with strong thread and tied up before dyeing.

Gutta is a resist medium that you can buy ready to use in tubes fitted with a nozzle for easy application. Once dry, it prevents the paint or dye in adjacent areas of the design from running together as you apply them. Gutta is a thin, glue-like substance that is available in a few different colours. Clear gutta washes out of fabric, but coloured lines will remain on the fabric and must be incorporated into the design.

Left: The background of this landscape has been hand-dyed, then sympathetically hand- and machine-embroidered.

Stamping techniques

Blocks used for stamping are available in different ready made shapes and sizes. Many of the larger stamps are made from a firm foam material, which is available from craft stores. It can be cut to any shape and glued on to a wood block ready for use.

Try the stamp out on spare paper and then on a small piece of fabric first. It may help to wash the background fabric before stamping to remove any fabric finish, or you can try adding a drop of detergent to the paint.

1 Use a paintbrush or sponge roller to apply a thin layer of acrylic paint over the stamp surface. Paint parts of the stamp in different colours or blend the paints over the stamp.

2 Place the stamp face down on the fabric and press. Avoid agitating the stamp as this will produce a blurred edge. Once dry, press the fabric on the wrong side to set the paint.

Colour washing

This is a simple method of applying colour to a background fabric with a sponge or brush. The finished result is difficult to control because the colour spreads over the fabric very much of its own accord.

However, wonderful effects can be achieved as one colour merges into another. Apply the paint straight from the bottle, or water it down to a paler shade before use. Colour washing can also be used to colour canvas for counted-thread embroidery. When coloured to match the wool (yarn), the canvas will be less obvious behind loose or openly worked stitches.

1 Wash the fabric to remove any sizing. Either apply the dye to wet fabric or iron the fabric dry before use. The moisture will help the dye to spread but will also dilute the colour. Apply the dye with a small sponge or paintbrush. Experiment with different-sized brushes for different effects.

2 Apply the next colour in the same way. Paint directly over the edge of the previous colour, or allow the colours to merge across a small gap. Colour washing is particularly suitable for creating sky, landscapes and garden designs.

Masking techniques

Using a media such as plastic or tape will prevent paint or dye from penetrating defined areas of the fabric.

1 Stick strips of masking tape to the background fabric to create the shapes you want. Make sure the tape is firmly stuck down to prevent the paint from seeping underneath.

2 Use stencil crayons or paints to fill in the uncovered areas between the strips of tape.

3 When working with a stencil brush or small sponge, make sure the excess paint is blotted off before applying it to the fabric.

Transferring a design

Embroidery designs can be transferred on to a background fabric in several ways. Which method you choose will depend on the fabric and thread (floss) you are using and the design. Some designs are simply outlined and then developed as you stitch, whereas others need all the fine details included from the start. Make sure that all marked lines will be covered with embroidery, even if you are using a vanishing-ink pen.

Direct tracing

This is the easiest way to transfer a design on to fabric but will only work on thin, light-coloured fabrics.

1 On light-coloured paper, draw your choice of design using a black felt tip pen.

2 Place the fabric over the design on a clean, flat surface. Re-draw the lines with a soft pencil.

Transfer pen

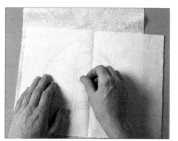

1 Ink from a transfer pen will not show up on dark fabrics so it is only suitable for lighter fabrics. This special pen is sold in kit form with the transfer paper. Using the pen, trace a mirror image of the design directly on to the transfer paper.

2 Place the fabric right side up on a hard surface. Position the transfer paper drawing side down on the fabric and rub along the lines with the edge of your thumbnail. (Some pens need the heat of an iron – use the manufacturer's instructions.)

3 Lift one corner of the transfer paper to check that the design has been transferred. If not, go over the lines again, pressing slightly harder.

Dressmaker's carbon

This method is best for firm, smooth fabrics. Choose a carbon colour to match the fabric – white carbon will show up on white fabric as a dull line.

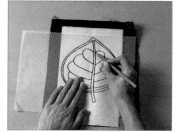

1 Place the fabric right side up on a hard surface. Cover with a piece of dressmaker's carbon, coloured side down. Position the design on top and draw along the lines with a blunt pencil.

2 Check that the lines have been transferred clearly before removing the carbon.

Prick-and-pounce

This traditional transfer method is suitable for all fabric types. It works best with simple designs.

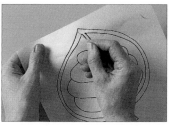

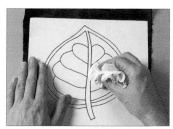

MAKING A POUNCE BAG

Cut two squares of muslin, each 15cm/6in, and place one on top of the other. Place a tablespoon of cornflour (cornstarch) in the centre and draw up the raw edges to make a bag.

1 Draw the design on a firm sheet of paper. Make small holes along the lines with a thick needle, or stitch along the lines using an unthreaded sewing machine. Place the fabric right side up on a hard surface.

2 Rub the muslin bag over the surface to push the cornflour (cornstarch) through the holes. Check that the design has been transferred. Baste or draw along the lines to make the design more permanent.

Using a hoop or frame

For most embroidery you will need to stretch the fabric in a hoop or frame to get the best result. A wooden hoop is the most popular. It is ideal for all types of embroidery, except those worked on canvas because canvas is damaged when crushed between the rings of the hoop.

Binding a hoop

Bind the inner hoop with tape before you begin. Wrap a length of 5mm/¼in wide seam tape round the inside ring at a slight angle so that the tape overlaps all the way round. Fold the raw edge to the inside of the hoop and hem stitch in place.

Fitting the fabric in the hoop

Remove the outer frame and place the stitching area of the fabric, right side up, over the inner hoop. Hold the outer ring in place and push down to secure the fabric between the rings. Loosen the tension ring slightly on a thicker fabric before pushing it into place. If the fabric isn't taut in all directions, tighten the screw slightly and re-fit. Use a screwdriver to tighten the outer hoop to keep the tension taut. If the fabric works loose or needs moving, lift the hoop off without loosening the screws and re-fit. Avoid permanently stretching the fabric. Fine fabric can be stretched over a firm lightweight backing fabric, then stretched in the hoop and worked as a single fabric.

RECTANGULAR FRAMES

• Rotary frames are used to embroider a long piece. The area being worked on can be placed between the two bars and stitched to fabric attached to each side of the bar. This involves more time-consuming preparation, but for large pieces of work it is worth the effort, since your work will be held taut without the need to readjust it.

• Interlocking-bar frames are made of four wood bars that fit together. The fabric is stretched and secured in place with staples or drawing pins. This is a quicker method of preparation, suitable for smaller pieces of work.

Outline and composite stitches

Contemporary designs often use traditional embroidery stitches in an innovative way. But before experimenting with different stitches you need to know how to work a whole range of stitches.

Many outline stitches will be familiar to you as they are the basic stitches used in hand embroidery. Composite stitches are made up of two outline stitches, with further embellishment added.

Feather stitch

The Victorians often used this delicate stitch on their crazy patchwork because its light, feathery line contrasted beautifully with the heavy, ornate fabrics they used. It can be worked as a straight or a gently curving line.

Work slanting stitches alternately to the left and to the right. Tuck the working thread (floss) under the needle before pulling it through.

Double feather stitch

Double feather stitch forms a wide branched line that can be worked in a soft curve. It creates a delicate lacy effect when used as a filling stitch.

It is worked in the same way as feather stitch, except several stitches are made to each side before changing direction. You can either work an equal number of stitches on each side or vary the amount to create an undulating line.

Closed feather stitch

Closed feather stitch is worked in a straight line singly or in multiple rows. It is effective when used to couch narrow ribbon or braid.

Bring the needle out on one side, near the top of the stitching line. Take a straight stitch across to the opposite stitching line. Bring the needle out slightly further down this stitching line, pulling the working thread over the previous stitch as shown. Work from side to side in this way.

Coral stitch

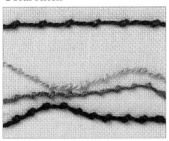

Coral stitch is a thin line stitch that has tiny knots evenly spaced along its length. Change the spacing and position of the knots in each row to create different textural effects.

Work from right to left. Take a small stitch where the next knot is to be formed. Loop the thread (floss) around the needle and hold the knot in place with your thumb as you pull the needle through the fabric.

Knotted cable stitch

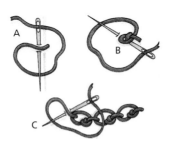

Knotted cable stitch is a combination of cable and coral stitches. Although it looks quite complicated, it is stitched in stages and the coral stitch holds the chain loop in place while the next stitch is worked.

Begin by making a coral stitch (A). Push the needle into the fabric under this stitch and work a chain stitch (B). Continue alternating between coral and chain stitches (C).

Scroll stitch

Scroll stitch looks like tiny waves. It is ideal for intricate shapes. The closer the scrolls are worked, the tighter the curve. Use a round thread for a raised effect or stranded cotton for a wide, flat line.

Work the stitch from left to right. Take a small stitch and loop the thread around the needle. Pull the needle through and begin the next stitch further to the right.

Double knot stitch

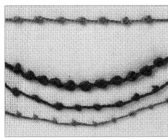

Double knot stitch makes a beaded line and is best worked in a round thread to make neat raised knots. Use it for areas of surface texture.

Working from left to right, make a small diagonal straight stitch across the stitching line (A). Slip the needle under the previous long straight stitch and pull the thread through. Feed the needle under and over the stitch threads and bring the needle out over the working thread ready to begin the next double knot (B).

Chain stitch

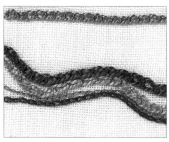

Chain stitch is one of the most popular embroidery stitches. It can be worked in a single line, in a spiral or in multiple rows to fill shapes.

Work the stitch as shown in the diagram, making each loop a similar size. Any embroidery thread (floss) suitable for the fabric can be used, but a smooth thread shows the loops well. Finish the chain by making a tiny straight stitch through the last loop.

Chequered chain stitch

Chequered chain stitch is a decorative line stitch worked in two colours.

Thread the needle with two coloured threads and bring them out on the right side. Work a chain stitch, looping only one of the colours to form the chain under the needle. Pull the needle through until the chain is formed. Tug the other coloured thread gently to pull the excess thread to the wrong side.

Twisted chain stitch

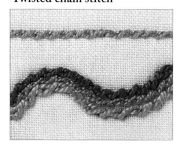

Twisted chain stitch is simple to stitch and looks effective when the stitches are small. A round thread produces a raised line, while stranded cotton has a flatter look.

Bring the needle up through the fabric and hold the thread down with your left thumb close to where it emerges from the fabric. Work a small chain stitch over the thread, using the illustration as a guide.

Double chain stitch

Double chain stitch is a simple variation of chain stitch that forms a wide band. It is generally worked in a straight line or in rows to fill large spaces, but can be stitched in a gentle curve. You can also alter the width of the double chain stitch to fill the space between two wavy lines. Perfect the chain stitch first before trying this more decorative stitch.

Begin at the top left. Work wide chain stitches alternately to the left and to the right, as shown.

Feathered chain stitch

Feathered chain stitch is a variation of chain stitch. Rows of feathered chain stitch can be worked side by side as a diamond or irregular filling stitch, or overlapped in a random fashion to build texture.

Make a diagonal chain stitch then make a small diagonal stitch downwards from right to left, ready to work the chain stitch on the other side. Continue down the fabric.

Heavy chain stitch

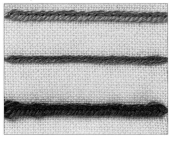

Heavy chain stitch makes a bold line that is ideal for heavy outlines.

Make a straight stitch and bring the needle out further down the line. Thread the needle under the straight stitch and back through the fabric where it emerged. Bring the needle out further down and work a second loop through the straight stitch. Continue down the row, but thread the needle under the previous loops.

Whipped chain stitch

Whipped chain stitch makes a heavy raised line that is useful for strong outlines. The stitch will be bolder if whipped in both directions. You can also whip each side of the chain with more than one colour.

Work a row of chain stitches. Thread a tapestry needle with a contrasting or matching thread (floss), and whip under each chain stitch without sewing into the fabric.

Cable stitch

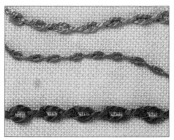

Cable stitch works equally well as a line or a filling stitch. The stitch can easily be worked along a curve. Rows of cable stitches can be joined with small straight stitches or whipped together.

Begin with an ordinary chain stitch, then wrap the thread around the needle as shown before making a short straight stitch and bringing the needle back out of the fabric to make the next chain. Pass the thread under the point of the needle before pulling it through to form the loop.

Back stitch

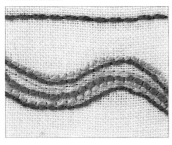

Back stitch is a fine line stitch that can be curved or angular, depending on the length of the stitches. Try using different weights of thread (floss).

Work back stitch from right to left, inserting the needle at the end of the previous stitch. Bring it back out at the start of the next stitch. Keep each stitch the same size and avoid pulling the thread tight or leaving it loose.

Whipped back stitch

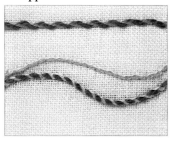

Whipped back stitch can be worked in one colour to create a heavy line resembling fine cord, or in contrasting colours for a decorative effect. Try using a different weight of thread for the back stitch and the whip stitch.

Work a row of 5mm/¼in long back stitches. Thread a needle with another colour or weight of thread and slip it under each back stitch without going into the fabric.

Threaded back stitch

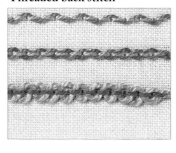

Threaded back stitch can be worked in one or several different threads. Choose a smooth thread for the back stitch, and fancy or metallic threads to weave through.

Work a row of small back stitches. Thread a needle with the second colour and slip the needle under each back stitch, alternately up and down, without going into the fabric. Work a third thread in the opposite direction.

Stem stitch

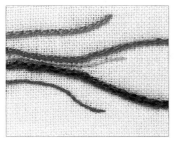

Stem stitch is one of the most common line stitches. It is used to fill in small areas of a design if the stitches are small and evenly sized.

Stem stitch is worked in a similar motion to back stitch, only from left to right. Work up the thread line keeping the thread loop to the right of the needle, and bringing the needle back out half-way down the previous stitch. Aim to make the stitches look like a smooth line and all the same size.

Split stitch

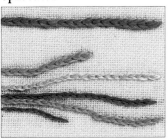

Split stitch is used for creating lines or when worked in rows, as a filling stitch. It is best suited to stitching details such as hands, feet and faces. When stitched correctly, split stitch looks like a fine chain stitch.

Split stitch is worked in a similar way to stem stitch except the needle is brought up through the middle of the previous stitch, using the point of the needle to split the thread (floss).

Pekinese stitch

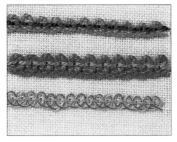

Pekinese stitch can be worked as a line stitch or as a solid filling stitch. Use a fine thread for the foundation row, and a heavier-weight thread to create a braid-like effect.

Work a row of back stitches loosely across the fabric. Thread a tapestry needle with the second colour and loop it through each back stitch as shown. Tighten each loop as it forms and keep them even along the rows.

Running stitch

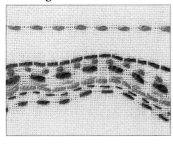

Running stitch can be a tiny prick stitch, a line of basting or a near-solid line, depending on the length of the stitches and the spacing between each. In embroidery, running stitch is worked as a single line or in multiple rows to fill larger areas.

Take the needle in and out across the fabric. Several stitches can be "run" on the needle at one time before it is pulled through the fabric.

Whipped running stitch

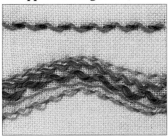

Whipped running stitch or cordonnet stitch is a raised line stitch used for outlines and fine details. Work a subtle line in two shades of the same colour or create a decorative line with two contrasting colours.

Work a line of even running stitches, leaving a gap between each stitch. Aim to make the gaps the same length as each stitch. Use a blunt tapestry needle to whip a second thread neatly and evenly through each stitch.

Cretan stitch

Cretan stitch is a long-armed feather stitch that is often used as a border pattern. It can be used singly or in rows as a filling stitch.

Begin at the top of the centre stitching line. Make long stitches down the fabric, slanting them alternately to the left and to the right. Loop the thread (floss) under the needle each time before pulling it through.

Open Cretan stitch

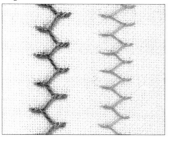

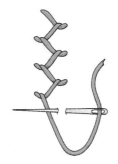

Open Cretan stitch can be worked in a straight or a gently curving line. Several rows side by side form a delicate honeycomb pattern.

Work in the same way as Cretan stitch. Keep the needle horizontal and take a small stitch towards the centre line. Pull the needle through over the working thread. Work a series of stitches alternately to the left and right down the fabric.

Closed Cretan stitch

Closed Cretan stitch is generally used to fill small shapes such as leaves. It can also be worked between two straight lines as a heavy, braid-like border stitch. A flat thread such as stranded cotton gives the best coverage when working solid shapes, but a round thread is better for the border stitch.

Draw out the shape on the fabric with a vanishing-ink pen. Working from alternate sides, take small stitches in towards the centre of the shape as shown. Pull the needle out over the working thread.

Left: Cretan stitch would traditionally be used as a border on soft furnishing items such as tablecloths, or on clothes.

Cross stitch

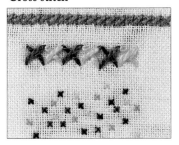

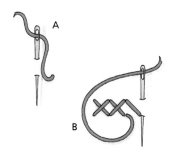

Cross stitch is one of the oldest and most common embroidery stitches. It can be worked individually or in rows, but it is essential to make the top half of each stitch slant in the same direction for an even result.

To work a row of cross stitches, first sew a line of diagonal stitches (A), then complete each cross with a second diagonal stitch on the return journey (B).

Couching

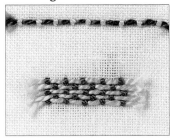

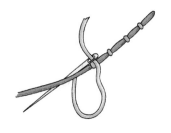

Couching is used to attach groups of thread (floss) to fabric.

Hold the thread to be couched with your thumb. Working from right to left, take small stitches across the bulky thread. Make the couching stitches close together when working a curve and secure a corner with several stitches. Use a large-eyed needle to take the couched thread through to the wrong side.

Pendant couching

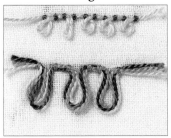

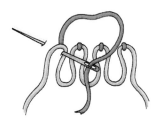

Rows of pendant couching stitched one above the other form a loop-pile filling stitch. Try cutting the loops to create a tufted texture.

Working from right to left, hold the thread to be couched with your left thumb. Work a small stitch across it, then form the base thread into a loop. Couch the other side of the loop. Continue along the stitching line, forming small loops between pairs of couching stitches.

Satin stitch couching

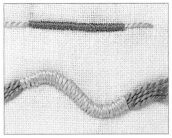

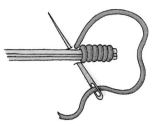

Satin stitch couching forms a neat raised line that is ideal for strong outlining. Here the couched threads are completely hidden by the embroidery thread.

Place a thick thread, or a bundle of threads, across the fabric and couch it down with small touching stitches that completely cover the threads. Use a large-eyed needle to pull the couched threads through to the wrong side at the end.

Band and border stitches

These are usually worked in straight lines or gentle curves to create borders or fillings, but there is plenty of scope for innovation. Traditionally they were used to bind the edges of items such as blankets and tablecloths. Experiment using different threads (floss) or work parts of the stitch in a different scale to change the appearance. Stitch several different bands together to create an unusual wide border.

Buttonhole stitch and blanket stitch

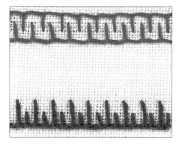

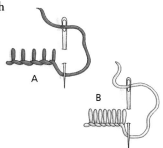

Buttonhole and blanket stitch are essentially the same, except for the way they are spaced. The space between each blanket stitch matches the length of the vertical stitch (A). With buttonhole stitch, the stitches are worked close together (B).

Work both types of stitch from left to right. Space them as required, pulling the needle through over the top of the working thread (floss).

Double buttonhole stitch

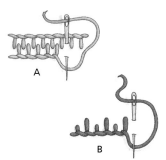

This should more correctly be called double blanket stitch because it consists of two facing rows of blanket stitches worked as a band (A). Long and short buttonhole stitch is another variation in which the stitches are alternately long and short (B).

Work a row of blanket stitches from left to right, then turn the fabric around and work a second facing row from left to right. Position the vertical stitches in the gaps between those of the previous row.

Knotted buttonhole stitch

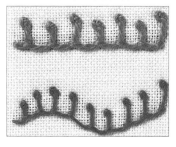

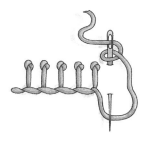

Knotted buttonhole stitch is a pretty variation of blanket stitch. Use a round thread to enhance the raised appearance of the stitch.

Working from left to right, wind the thread over your left thumb and drop the loop on to the fabric so that the tail is underneath. Push the needle through the loop and make a blanket stitch. Tug the loop tight before pulling the needle through.

Closed buttonhole stitch

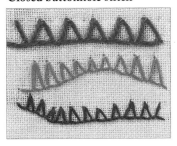

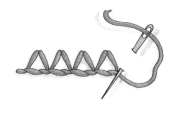

Closed buttonhole stitch is a variation of blanket stitch. Rows of stitching can be worked back-to-back or interlocking, to form a range of borders or filling patterns.

Work the first blanket stitch at an angle and then work the second stitch into the same hole to make a triangle. Try working three or even four threads (floss) into the same holes for a more complex result.

Ladder stitch

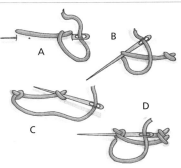

Use ladder stitch for straight borders and for filling long, straight shapes.

Bring the needle out at the top left, take it across to the right-hand side and make a small stitch (A). Stitch back across from right to left as shown. Without stitching through the fabric, make a knot on the left-hand side (B) and again on the right-hand side (C). Work down the fabric in this way to form a ladder (D).

Diamond stitch

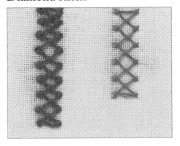

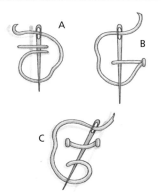

Diamond stitch forms a wide lacy border between two parallel lines.

Make a stitch from left to right then bring the needle out just below on the right-hand side. Make a knot at the end (A). Take the thread across and make another knot on the left-hand side (B). Insert the needle just under the knot and bring it out further down the line. Make a knot in the centre (C). Take a small vertical stitch on the right-hand side and continue to form the diamond.

Vandyke stitch

Vandyke stitch is a wide ladder stitch that has an attractive plaited (braided) line down the middle.

Bring the needle out on the left-hand side and take a back stitch in the centre, slightly higher up. Work a stitch from right to left through the fabric. Then take the needle back under the previous stitch at the centre. Continue stitching through the fabric and under the stitch as shown.

Herringbone stitch

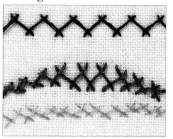

Herringbone stitch forms a crossed zigzag and makes an open border.

Working from left to right, bring the needle up through the fabric. Make a small stitch from right to left, slightly ahead and above. Move down to the lower line and work a second small stitch from right to left, ahead of your last stitch. Continue to alternate between the upper and lower guidelines.

Threaded herringbone stitch

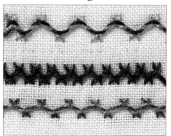

Threaded herringbone stitch produces a zigzag or solid border. Multiple rows of this stitch can be used as a very ornate filling stitch.

First, work a row of herringbone stitch. Then, starting on the left-hand side, use a tapestry needle to slip the second thread (floss) first under and then over at the point where the herringbone stitches form a cross. Do not pull the thread tight.

Fancy herringbone stitch

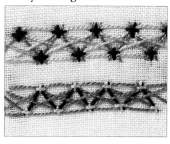

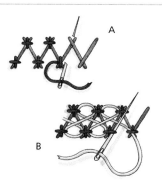

Fancy herringbone stitch is an elaborate border stitch.

Mark parallel lines on plain fabric. Make a foundation row of herring-bone stitches, widely spaced. Work an upright cross stitch over each of the top and bottom intersections, making the vertical bar of the cross before the horizontal bar (A). Work the interlacing loops (B), using the illustration as a guide.

Laced herringbone stitch

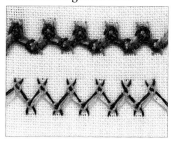

Work laced herringbone stitch in a hoop to prevent the foundation row from being pulled out of shape.

Work a row of herringbone stitches 2cm/³⁄₄in wide. Turn the work upside down. Working from left to right around the crossed part of the herringbone stitch, lace the thread under and over the foundation and the stitching thread as you cross it. Make two circles around the top crosses and one-and-a-half times around each lower cross.

Tied herringbone stitch

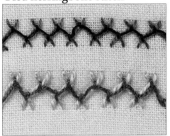

Tied herringbone stitch makes a knotted zigzag line and is usually worked in two contrasting colours. It is used as a border design or in multiple rows as a filling stitch.

Work a row of herringbone stitches. Without picking up the background, use a different thread (floss) to sew a row of coral stitches over the top. Place each coral stitch where the herringbone stitches cross.

Double herringbone stitch

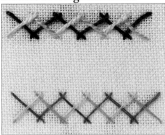

Double herringbone stitch is also used as a foundation for more complicated border stitches.

Work a row of herringbone stitches. Work a second row on top in the gaps between the stitches. You can interlace the stitches if you wish by threading the needle under the foundation row on the upward stitch, and running the thread over it on the downward stitch.

Interlaced herringbone stitch

Interlaced herringbone stitch makes an elaborate border stitch.

Work a foundation row of double herringbone stitches as shown. Bring the interlacing thread up on the left and take it around the first top cross. Lace across the top half of the herringbone stitches. Take the thread around the centre cross at the end of the row, then work back along the lower half to complete the stitch.

Chevron stitch

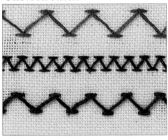

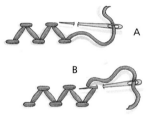

A

B

Chevron stitch looks similar to herringbone stitch. It is commonly used in smocking to make diamonds.

Bring the needle out through the fabric. Make a diagonal stitch, bringing the needle out a short distance back (A). Take a stitch along the line, ending ahead of the diagonal. Work a back stitch, bringing the needle back out next to the diagonal (B). Work the next diagonal stitch across to the lower line, bringing the needle out further back along the line as before.

Raised stitches

These stitches are usually made up of two or more stitches to create height. They are used in three-dimensional stumpwork and other ornate embroidery techniques. The stitches illustrated here are composite band stitches, meaning that they each travel in a line and are made up of more than one stitch or layer of stitching. They are ideal for making use of different threads (floss) and colours.

Raised chevron stitch

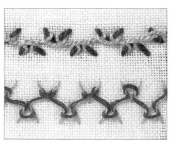

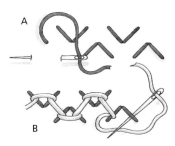

This makes a strong, raised line, and is used for borders and in multiple rows to make deep bands.

Stitch a foundation row of V-shaped stitches from right to left in a back stitch motion (A). Thread a needle with the second thread (floss) and bring it through at the top left of the foundation (B). Work the stitches across the foundation without catching the background fabric.

Raised chain band

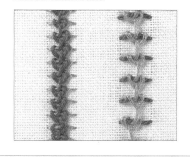

Work raised chain band in a hoop. Try making the bars and chains in different weights of thread.

Work a row of small horizontal stitches. Bring the needle out just above the centre of the top horizontal stitch. Slip the needle over the bar to emerge at the left. Insert the needle under the bar at the right to form a loop. Take the needle under the bar below and pull it through the loop.

Raised stem stitch band

Raised stem stitch band is a dense raised band that forms a distinctive long oval shape and is used as a feature on heavy embroidery.

Stitch a foundation block of long straight stitches close together, and to the required width. Work a series of parallel straight stitches across the foundation. Thread a tapestry needle with thread, and bring it out at the base of the block. Work stem stitches over the horizontal threads. Continue until the foundation is covered.

Striped woven band

This stitch is used for filling and borders. Work with two different-coloured threads (floss).

Work a foundation band of evenly spaced horizontal straight stitches. Thread two needles and bring both threads through at the top left above the first stitch. Weave the threads alternately over and under the foundation. Begin each row with the same colour.

Raised lattice band

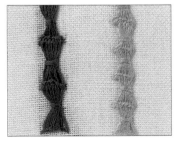

This is a pretty, compact border stitch. It can be worked in different weights and colours of thread. Work with the fabric held in a hoop or frame.

Work a foundation of long straight stitches, putting more in the centre to create a rounded appearance. Cover the foundation layer with closely worked satin stitches. Work a row of threaded herringbone stitches over the satin stitches.

Sheaf stitch

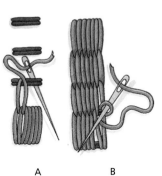

A   B

This is an unusual border stitch.

Stitch a foundation of pairs of horizontal straight stitches. Work satin stitches over the bottom two pairs. Work subsequent vertical satin stitches, taking the needle between the previous stitches (A). Stitch between the first two satin stitches, one from above and one from below. Slip the needle through the loop (B). Tighten to make a knot. Work a knot between each pair of stitches. Work two satin stitches to gather the "sheafs".

Right: This stitch sampler makes innovative use of traditional band stitches and is an inspirational way of displaying stitches.

When you are learning new stitches, rather than working rows and rows of neat lines, add interest to your work with different weights of threads (floss) and unusual textures.

Edging and insertion stitches

Edging stitches are used to finish hemmed edges or to add a decorative border to appliqué. Insertion stitches are used to join two pieces of fabric to make an open decorative seam. This technique was originally used to make large pieces of table linen from long narrow strips of fabric. Insertion stitches are traditionally worked in white on white and are a delicate feature on christening and bridal wear.

Looped edging stitch

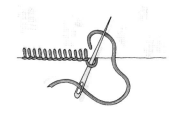

Work looped edging stitch from left to right over a small turned edge. This stitch looks like buttonhole stitch.

Secure the thread (floss) close to the edge on the wrong side. Insert the needle from the back of the fabric at the edge. Pull the thread through and take the needle through the loop from the back, going over the working thread. Pull the knot tight.

Venetian picot stitch

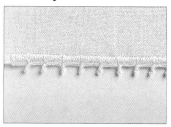

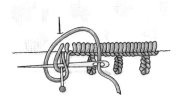

Venetian picot stitch is used to decorate a plain buttonhole edging.

Work a few buttonhole stitches. Insert a pin through the fold next to the last stitch. Loop the thread under the pin and begin another buttonhole stitch, carrying the thread around the pin. Weave the needle under the loop thread, over the pin and under the other loop thread. Make sure you go over the working thread. Pull to tighten the knot. Work buttonhole stitch all the way down the loop.

Antwerp edging stitch

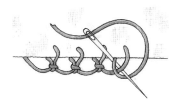

Antwerp edging stitch is worked on plain fabric as a loose, decorative knotted edging.

Work the stitch from left to right. Bring the needle through on the fold. Make a buttonhole stitch. Hold the working thread under your thumb next to the stitch. Slip the needle behind the stitches and over the working thread. Pull the knot tight and continue along the edge.

Interlaced insertion stitch

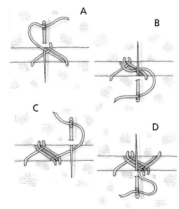

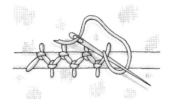

This stitch has a pretty, lacy look.

Hem stitch two strips of fabric then baste both on to a strip of brown paper, leaving at least a 5mm/¹⁄₄in gap between them. Bring the needle through the bottom fold at the left-hand side. Take a small stitch diagonally to the right through the front of the upper fold (A). Take another stitch to the right along the bottom fold, then back to the top fold (B). Loop the needle around the previous stitch to make a twist (C) before inserting it along the top fold from behind (D).

Knotted insertion stitch

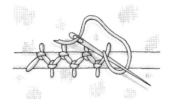

Knotted insertion stitch is slightly heavier than interlaced stitch and has pretty knots instead of twists. The gap between the two fabrics can be slightly wider.

Prepare the fabrics by hemming and basting them on to a strip of brown paper about 9mm/³⁄₈in apart. The knots are the same as those used in Antwerp edging. Begin at the left-hand side, working the stitches alternately on the top and bottom fabric edges. Once complete, remove the basting and brown paper, and press gently on the wrong side.

Looped edge insertion stitch

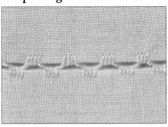

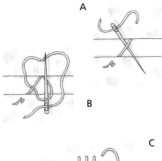

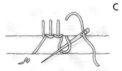

Looped edge insertion stitch makes a firm, narrow join with a delicate appearance (A). The same effect can be achieved with both knotted (B) and regular buttonhole stitch (C). The looped edge stitch is simple to work.

Hem and baste the two pieces of fabric to a strip of brown paper about 5mm/¹⁄₄in apart. Begin at the right-hand side and work groups of four looped edge stitches alternately on the top and bottom fabric edges. The effect can be altered by using different numbers of stitches or by changing the gap between the fabric edges.

Carefully remove the basting stitches holding the brown paper to the work.

Isolated stitches

Isolated stitches are very versatile. The smaller ones can be used individually to add details such as eyes, berries and flower centres, or they can be scattered in a random fashion to fill in a large background. They can also be used to create texture on top of other stitches. Larger isolated stitches are useful for heavier embroidery techniques. Experiment with thread (floss) and colour combinations until you get the desired effect.

Bullion knots

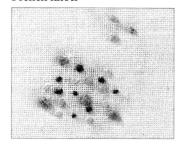

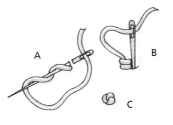

Use a long needle with a small eye to work bullion knots.

Bring the needle out at A and make a back stitch the required length of the knot (B). Bring the needle back out at A. Coil the thread (floss) round the needle seven times then pull the needle through the coil. Hold the coil down with the left thumb, pull the working thread to make the coil lie flat, then insert the needle at C.

French knots

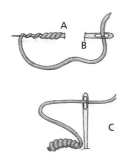

French knots add texture and colour when scattered over fabric and can also be used *en masse* to fill a shape with subtle shading and rich texture.

Bring the needle and thread up through the fabric. Take a small stitch where the thread emerged. Twist the thread around the needle twice (A) then gently pull the needle through (B). Stitch back through the fabric at the side of the knot (C).

Straight stitch

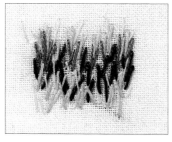

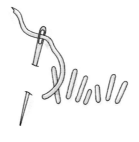

Straight stitch is quick to work and useful for covering large areas with texture. Add shading by stitching in various tones of the same colour, or by using several colours of fine thread in the needle at one time.

Work individual straight stitches over the fabric, varying the size and direction at will. Overlap the stitches to create areas of dense texture.

Fly stitch

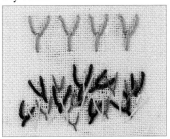

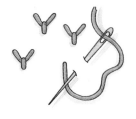

Fly stitch can be worked individually, or in rows as an evenly spaced filling. Vary the length of the tail to produce different effects.

Bring the needle through the fabric at the top left of the stitch, and insert it through the fabric diagonally from the top right as shown. Pull the needle through over the working thread (floss) and make a vertical stitch or tail to hold the loop in place.

Lazy daisy stitch

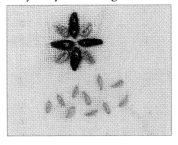

Lazy daisy stitch is a single chain stitch caught down with a small straight stitch at one end. Stitch it in rows or scatter the stitches to create texture. Most threads are suitable, but varying the weight of the thread will alter the size of stitch.

Work lazy daisy stitch in the same way as chain stitch, but anchor each loop with a small straight stitch before beginning the next loop.

Lazy daisy with straight stitch

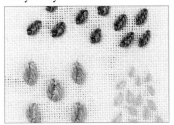

This variation of lazy daisy stitch is more solid and looks like tiny leaves or solid petals. It can be worked alongside lazy daisy stitch to vary the texture, scattered randomly over the fabric, or stitched in a flower shape.

Work a lazy daisy stitch, then add a straight stitch down the centre. Use contrasting colours for leaves or different weights of thread for a solid effect.

Long-tailed lazy daisy stitch

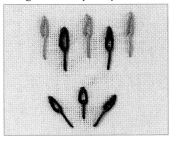

Long-tailed lazy daisy stitch can be worked in a circle, with the straight stitches pointing inwards or outwards, to make a flower. Work the stitches side by side or with the loops arranged alternately at the top and bottom of the row.

Work the stitch in the same way as lazy daisy stitch, but add an extended anchoring stitch to create the tail.

Woven wheel

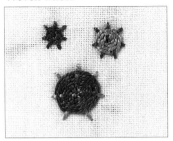

Woven wheels make attractive raised circular motifs for spiders' webs or large flowers.

Work an odd number of evenly-spaced straight stitches, usually seven or nine, radiating from the centre of a circle. Weave a second thread (floss) over and under the straight stitches, starting in the centre and working out. Use a tapestry needle to avoid catching the straight threads.

Ribbed wheel

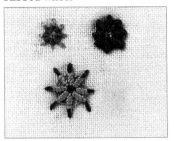

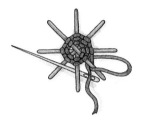

Ribbed wheels are a variation of woven wheels, forming a textured circle with pronounced radiating bars. They look best worked in a round thread with a sheen, such as coton perlé.

Work an even number of straight stitches radiating from the centre of a circle. Eight and 12 are the most common arrangements. Then work back stitches over the spokes, spiralling out from the centre. Use a tapestry needle to avoid picking up the fabric.

Buttonhole wheel

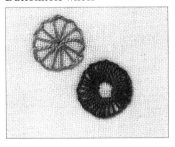

A buttonhole wheel is a circular version of buttonhole stitch. On loose-weave fabrics, the stitches can go through the same point in the centre to make a decorative eyelet.

Work buttonhole stitches closely together, leaving a small circle in the centre, and add French knots to the centre. Alternatively, arrange the stitches so that each straight stitch goes into the same hole in the centre.

Catherine wheel

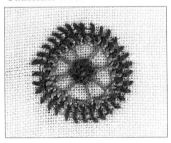

A Catherine wheel was originally an open needlepoint filling stitch. Use a firm round thread.

Work a large circle of blanket stitches, with the straight bars fanning outwards. Work a second row of blanket stitches through the loops of the first circle, using a tapestry needle. Work four straight stitches across the centre, to make eight spokes. Work two rings of back stitch over the spokes at the centre.

Raised cup stitch

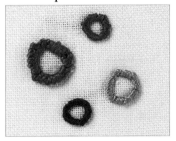

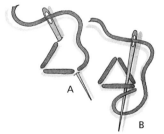

Raised cup stitch forms a heavy raised ring. It is used in stumpwork or Jacobean embroidery.

Stitch an equilateral triangle then bring the needle out at one corner (A). Take the needle under one side of the triangle and loop the working thread (floss) around the needle before pulling through (B). Work these stitches along the side of the triangles without catching the fabric. Pack the stitches quite tightly.

Crow's foot

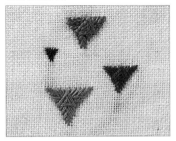

A crow's foot is a tailoring stitch used to strengthen a garment at the top of pleats or pockets. It can also be used as an embroidery stitch. Use a hoop or frame to keep the tension even.

Bring the thread out at the point where you want the base of the triangle to be. Make a long stitch to the top left corner of the triangle. Make a second stitch to the right-hand corner, ensuring it overlaps the first stitch slightly. Each stitch should be the same length. Continue around the triangle, working in to the centre so that the lines of stitching appear to interlock with each other.

Below: This impressionistic flower garden is made up of random isolated stitches in vibrant hues of colour.

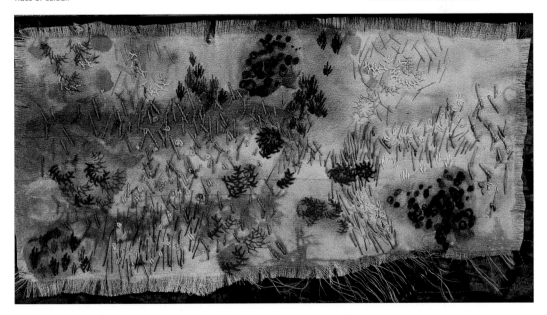

Filling stitches

Filling stitches can either be solid or open. Solid (filling) stitches cover the fabric completely and are generally worked over quite small areas. Although the stitches look quite simple, some, such as satin stitch, take practice to work neatly. Open filling stitches cover larger areas in a random or regulated way. Work open filling stitches with the fabric stretched in a hoop to keep the thread (floss) at the correct tension.

Brick stitch

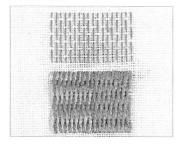

Brick stitch is easy to work and fills large spaces quickly. Rows of "bricks" can be worked in different colours to create subtle shading.

Work a row of straight stitches along the top edge of the area to be filled, making them alternately full- and half-length. Work back across the area, adding full-length stitches under the half stitches. Stagger the full-length stitches until the shape is full.

Basket filling stitch

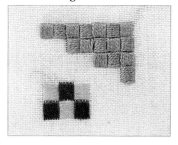

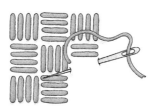

Basket filling stitch is best worked on even-weave fabrics. Although this stitch is traditionally worked in a single colour, an attractive chequerboard effect can be achieved by using two colours.

Basket filling stitch is usually worked by alternating blocks of four horizontal and four vertical satin stitches. The rows can be stitched in any direction, but the stitches should be of equal size and spacing.

Fishbone stitch

Fishbone stitch is a filling stitch, but can be used as a heavy border. Use stranded thread (floss) and pack the stitches tightly over the background.

Score a line down the centre of the shape to be filled. If it helps, work a small straight stitch down the centre line from the top of the shape. Then make slanting straight stitches from the edge to just over the centre line, working from side to side.

Satin stitch

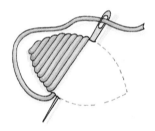

Satin stitch is a flat stitch that looks simple to work, but it takes practice to stitch it neatly. Blocks of stitches can be worked in different directions to create areas of light and shade.

Hold the fabric taut in a hoop. Work straight stitches across the shape, keeping them close together. Long satin stitches can look untidy, so choose an alternative stitch such as Romanian couching.

Padded satin stitch

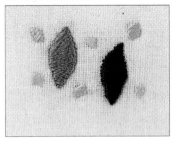

Padded satin stitch is slightly raised. It is used to emphasize shapes by making them stand out from flat areas of stitching. Work this stitch in an embroidery hoop to prevent the stitching from puckering the fabric.

Pad the shape with closely worked rows of running stitches, stem stitches or chain stitches. Then work satin stitch over the padding stitches. Keep the satin stitches close together.

Long and short stitch

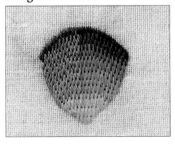

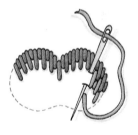

Long and short stitch is worked in the same way as satin stitch, although the finished appearance is completely different. Work this stitch in a hoop or frame.

Work the foundation row in alternate long and short satin stitches that follow the contours of the shape, completely covering the fabric with tightly packed straight stitches. Work rows of equal-sized stitches in this way until the shape is filled.

Left: These charming bird motifs are worked entirely by hand in long and short stitch.

Seeding

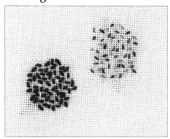

Seeding is a pretty filling stitch. Use single strands of cotton for a light, speckled filling. It can be used as padding under a solid filling stitch such as padded satin stitch. Use a single thread (floss) colour or several different colours for a mottled effect.

To work seeding, make tiny straight stitches randomly across the fabric area. Make them all the same length and packed closely together.

Open fishbone stitch

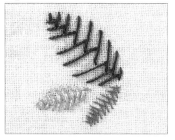

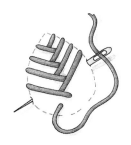

This is a variation of the solid fishbone stitch.

Bring the thread out just to the left of the centre line near the top and take a slanting stitch to the right edge. Bring the needle out on the left edge and work another slanting stitch that ends just to the right of the centre line. Continue until the shape is filled. An outline stitch around the edge will define the shape.

Roman filling stitch

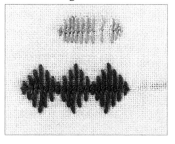

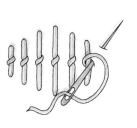

Roman filling stitch can be worked close together or widely spaced. It can also be worked in diamond shapes to create a regular mosaic-like pattern.

Work a long, straight stitch. Bring the needle out at the centre of the long stitch and make a short stitch over it. Either leave a space between each Roman filling stitch, or work them close together to cover the fabric area.

Leaf stitch

Leaf stitch is a light, open stitch. An outline stitch can be worked around the edge to define the shape.

Begin at the bottom, bringing the needle out to the left of the centre line. Working upwards, make a slanting stitch to the right-hand edge. Bring the needle out again near the centre line, below the first stitch and make another slanting stitch to the left-hand edge. Work slanting stitches until the shape is filled.

Detached wheat-ear stitch

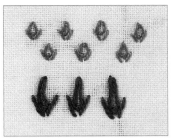

Work detached wheat-ear stitch in rows and grids, or as a scattering of isolated stitches. To keep the shape of the stitch in proportion, make larger stitches with a heavy thread (floss). The most striking effect is achieved with a thick, round thread such as coton perlé.

Work two straight stitches at right angles, in a "V" shape. Work a single daisy stitch over the base of the "V".

Tête de boeuf

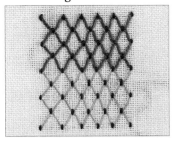

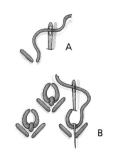

Tête de boeuf, or "bull's head", is a pretty stitch that can be used to make regular patterns or for random filling. The size of the stitch can be varied to create different effects. It can be worked very neatly on even-weave fabric if you count the threads.

Work two straight stitches at right angles (A), then place a single daisy stitch above (B). Position the next row between the previous stitches.

Cloud filling stitch

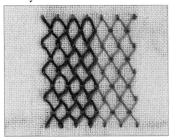

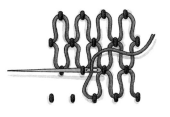

This light, lacy stitch can be used to fill shapes and cover backgrounds. Work the running stitches closer or further apart to alter the effect.

Work evenly spaced rows of small, vertical straight stitches in a diamond grid pattern as a foundation. Thread a tapestry needle with a contrasting colour and bring it out at the top right. Weave through each row of straight stitches in a zigzag pattern.

Fancy stitch

Fancy stitch is similar to cloud filling stitch, but creates a slightly different lacy trellis. Work it in two colours.

Work evenly spaced rows of alternate horizontal and vertical small straight stitches across the fabric. Thread a tapestry needle with a contrasting colour and bring it out top left. Weave down the fabric in a zigzag. Go under the working thread at the bottom before coming back up. Subsequent rows share the same horizontal and vertical stitches.

Roman filling burden stitch

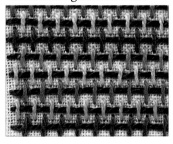

This is a couched filling stitch so the long straight stitches can be worked in fancy or decorative threads (floss). The short stitches are best worked in a smooth thread.

Work rows of evenly spaced long horizontal foundation stitches across the fabric. Couch these threads down with shorter vertical stitches. These stitches can be staggered in each row to form a brick pattern.

Trellis couching

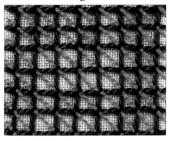

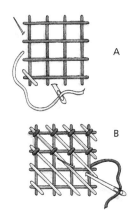

Trellis couching is built up from three layers of straight stitches that can be worked in similar or contrasting threads. It looks very effective when one of the long stitch layers is worked in metallic thread. Use an even-weave fabric for best results.

With the fabric held in a frame, work rows of long, evenly spaced horizontal straight stitches, then complete the grid with a series of similar vertical stitches. Add a third set of long straight stitches diagonally across the grid (A). Finally, anchor the threads with a small diagonal stitch across each intersection (B).

Square filling stitch 1

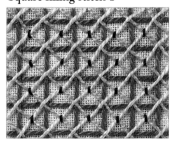

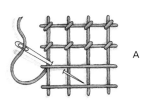

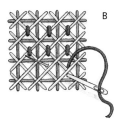

This makes a delicate square trellis pattern. It looks very effective if one of the long thread layers is sewn in metallic thread. This stitch is quite open when complete. Painting the background first will help the stitch if it is used in large quantities. To alter the effect, change the spacing of the stitches and use a different-weight thread.

Work rows of evenly spaced horizontal stitches, then complete the grid with a series of similar vertical stitches. Anchor the threads with a small diagonal stitch across each intersection (A). Sew a third and fourth set of long straight stitches diagonally across the square grid, as shown, and secure these with a short vertical stitch at each intersection as before (B).

Square filling stitch 2

This is a heavy, textured filling stitch worked on a diagonal grid. For best effect, use a metallic or fancy thread (floss) for the long diagonal stitches.

Work two pairs of long straight stitches to form a diagonal grid as in square filling stitch 1. Work an upright cross stitch at each intersection to anchor the long threads. Complete the pattern by working a French knot in the centre of each diamond.

Griffin stitch

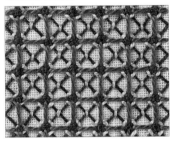

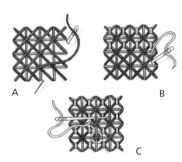

A   B

C

Griffin stitch forms an intricate multi-layered grid. It can be varied by changing the spacing of the stitches or the weight of the threads.

Work a square grid and then long straight stitches to form a diagonal grid as in square filling stitch 1 (A). Secure the diagonal threads by working a short straight stitch at each intersection (B). Thread a tapestry needle with the final thread and lace it around each intersection through all four long stitch layers (C).

Bokhara couching

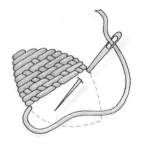

Use Bokhara couching to cover a background or to fill a shape. The same thread is used for both the laid stitches and the couching.

Begin at the left and work straight satin stitches across the area to be filled. Anchor them on the return journey with evenly spaced small slanting stitches. Stagger these stitches in each row. Only couch satin stitches when they are long enough.

Romanian couching

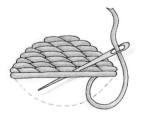

Romanian couching is worked in a similar way to Bokhara couching. Use it to cover a background or fill shapes.

Begin at the left and work long straight stitches across the area or shape. Secure the longer stitches on the return journey with evenly spaced long slanting stitches. It should be difficult to distinguish between the couched and the laid threads if this stitch is properly executed.

Cretan open filling stitch

This intricate-looking stitch creates a chequerboard effect. Stitch the first rows in a firm thread (floss). Use a supple thread for the overstitches.

Work evenly spaced vertical straight stitches across the area to be filled. Bring the second thread out at the top right corner. Sew blocks of Cretan stitches over the straight stitches, without picking up the background fabric.

Chevron stem stitch

This stitch looks like appliquéd tweed fabric. The straight horizontal stitches must be worked in a firm thread. Try using two colours.

Make a foundation of evenly spaced, long horizontal stitches. Bring a second thread out at the bottom left. Work stem stitches in a zigzag over the horizontal threads. The needle goes through the fabric at the beginning and end of each row.

Honeycomb filling stitch

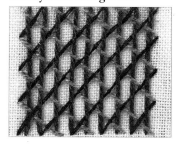

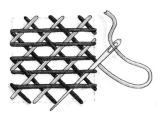

Honeycomb filling stitch is a geometric pattern made of three sets of interlocking straight stitches.

Work evenly spaced horizontal straight stitches across the area to be filled. Over the top of the work, stitch diagonally from bottom left to top right. Weave a third set of diagonal straight stitches in the opposite direction, passing the needle under the horizontal stitches and over the first set of diagonal stitches.

Ceylon stitch

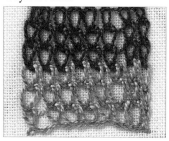

This is a needlelace stitch that can be worked very loosely to create a lacy filling, or tightly to look like knitting.

Make a straight stitch across the top of the area to be filled, and couch it down if it is quite long. Work evenly spaced loops from left to right over the thread, without catching the fabric. At the row end, take the thread down into the fabric and out a short distance below. Work the next row through the previous row.

Battlement couching

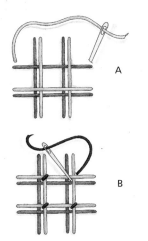

Battlement couching is an unusual filling for simple shapes. The stitch looks impressively complicated, but it is very simple to work. It can be worked in a single-colour thread (floss), but looks most effective when several shades of one colour are used.

Work two horizontal stitches with two vertical stitches on top in an offset cross formation (A). Continue adding pairs of horizontal and vertical stitches in this way, moving across one or two threads each time to create an overlapping lattice. Once complete, secure each intersection of the top four stitches with a small diagonal stitch (B).

Right: Couched threads (floss) and honeycomb filling stitch have been used to effect in this representational work.

Shisha work

Shisha are irregular pieces of mirror glass that are used extensively in Eastern embroidery. There are many different ways to attach shisha. Two methods are described here. Use an embroidery hoop to keep the fabric taut while attaching the shisha.

Method 1

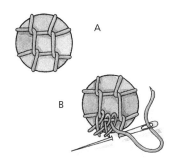

Use a strong thread (floss) that will not fray or break when pulled against the cut glass to work this traditional shisha embroidery stitch.

Create a frame for the embroidery stitches by sewing two threads across the shisha from side to side. Sew two more across the shisha, looping the thread around each laid thread (A). Bring the needle through to the right side close to the shisha. Take a stitch under the frame and cross over the first thread. Make a back stitch through the fabric (B). Continue around the shisha, bringing the needle up between the ends of the previous crossed loop.

Method 2

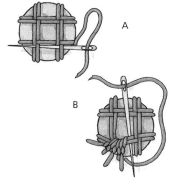

This is a pretty, ornate way to attach shisha. Work all the stitches the same length or make them alternately long and short, as shown.

Work eight straight stitches across the shisha, arranged in pairs. Take the last pair of stitches under the first pairs where they cross (A). Make the centre square small. Bring the needle out close to the shisha at the bottom left-hand corner and insert it close to where it emerged. Take a small stitch through the fabric and over the top of the working thread. Pull the thread towards the shisha to "set" the knot close to the edge of the glass. Take a second vertical stitch through the framework only (B).

Left: This antique piece of shisha work demonstrates the traditional method of applying glass, surrounded by vibrant colours in ornate hand embroidery.

Ribbon embroidery

Ribbon embroidery has existed in one form or another since the Middle Ages, but it was especially popular in Victorian times when frivolous, ornate embroidery techniques or "fancy work" were widely used. Flowers were a favourite theme, as they still are today.

Most embroidery stitches can be adapted for ribbon embroidery, but the stitches will look slightly different as the ribbon opens out on the surface. The simplest stitches are the most effective.

Ribbon embroidery looks deceptively difficult. In fact, the stitches used are either adapted straight stitches or well-known embroidery stitches such as daisy stitch, satin stitch and stem stitch. Narrow ribbon specially designed for

embroidery is available in different widths and a wide range of colours, made from either synthetic fibres or silk. Silk ribbons are more expensive but give wonderful results.

Almost any fabric can be used for ribbon embroidery, but it is easier to stitch on a looser weave. Linen and cotton even-weave fabrics are both suitable. Ribbon embroidery is a good technique for beginners, since the ribbon covers large areas quickly, and small designs can be finished quickly.

Threading a needle

Choose a needle that will allow the ribbon to pass through the fabric without fraying. Try out different-sized needles on the fabric to find the most suitable one. Don't worry too much if the needle makes a pronounced hole, because the ribbon should open out to cover it. Use this technique to secure the ribbon to a large needle to ensure it does not pull through the hole as you work.

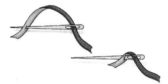

1 Thread the needle in the normal way then pierce the end of the ribbon with the needle as shown. Pull the long end to secure it over the eye. Work with short lengths so that the ribbon does not look ragged.

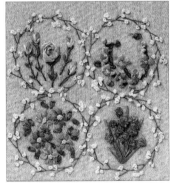

Beginning and finishing

1 To make a knot, first thread the needle in the normal way, then fold the end of the ribbon over the needle. Wrap the ribbon around the needle before pulling through.

2 Ribbon embroidery does not look very tidy on the wrong side, so finish the ribbon by threading under some of the ribbons on the wrong side.

Right: Ribbon embroidery lends itself to floral compositions and can be used with other embroidery techniques.

Garden flowers

Create your own herbaceous border using the flowers shown here. Fill in the spaces with simple leaves, worked in straight stitch in different greens.

Cornflower

Work one circle of straight stitches and a second over the top as shown. Stitch straight stitches to fill the centre. The leaves are ribbon stitch on a stem stitch stalk.

Hollyhock

Work in a cone shape. Begin at the top with green French knots then change to the flower colour. Make the French knots larger towards the base. Stitch French knots on top of the larger flowers, using thread (floss).

RIBBON STITCH

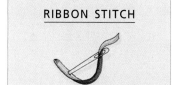

Bring the ribbon out and make a stitch directly through the ribbon.

Iris

Work one ribbon stitch vertically and three others in a fan below. The stalk is worked in stem stitch and the leaves in twisted straight stitch.

Hydrangea

Work four straight stitches for each flower and finish with a small French knot in the centre.

Periwinkle

Work five petals in short straight stitch then fill the centre with a French knot. The leaves are straight stitches and the buds are ribbon stitch.

Pansy

Work five ribbon stitches, two in yellow and three in purple. Add straight stitch stamens and a French knot to complete the centre.

Wild flowers

This pretty display of traditional wild flowers is worked in ribbon embroidery, with finer details in embroidery thread (floss).

Poppy

Work four to six loop stitches around a central French knot. Use a plastic drinking straw to make each loop the same size. Work a ring of black French knots around the centre.

Foxglove

Work a stem up to the top of the proposed flower tip. Work small green French knots in thread, then a few flower-colour ribbon French knots. Continue down with straight stitches, changing to ribbon stitch for the lower flowers.

Daisy

Work straight stitches out from the centre in palest blue. Fill the centre with tiny thread French knots.

Bluebell

Work three ribbon stitches for the flower, only pulling the ribbon until a roll appears at the bottom of each petal. Work two straight stitches on top for the calyx and then work a stem stitch stalk.

Buttercup

Work five loop stitches over a cocktail stitch in a circle. Work a large French knot in the centre and surround it with tiny French knots.

Snowdrop

Work three straight stitches in a fan shape, with a green French knot at the top. Work a green thread straight stitch at the tip of each petal.

Counted-thread embroidery

Cross stitch, blackwork and Assisi work are all counted-thread embroidery, and are stitched on even-weave embroidery fabrics such as linen or Aida. Even-weave means that there are an equal number of threads running horizontally and vertically throughout the fabric. Needlepoint, often wrongly called tapestry, is worked on open-weave canvas using wool (yarn).

Fabrics

Even-weave fabrics are available in various sizes, or counts. The count refers to the number of threads per square 2.5cm/1in.

Linen is a soft, high-quality plain-weave fabric. As the weave is quite fine, stitches are normally worked over two threads. Linen is an expensive fibre and many so-called linen fabrics are actually made from cotton or a mixture of fibres such as cotton, linen and viscose.

Aida is a 100 per cent cotton fabric woven from blocks of four threads with distinctive holes formed between each block. This makes Aida very easy to stitch on. It is available in a wide range of colours in 6 to 18 counts. Many Aida fabrics are only available in 14 count, the most popular size. You can also buy fancy fabrics, such as Lurex or Rustico, that have metallic or linen threads woven through them. The holes in these fabrics are slightly less pronounced than those on regular Aida.

Hardanger embroidery is also worked on even-weave fabric. It can be stitched on linen or on a 22-count Hardanger fabric that is woven in pairs of weft and warp threads.

Waste canvas, a loose, weave canvas, is used as a guide for working cross stitch on plain fabric. Once the cross stitch is complete, the canvas threads are loosened by spraying with water or by agitating the threads, and then removed with tweezers.

Plastic canvas is a non-fray material used for counted-thread embroidery. The finer gauge is ideal for cross-stitch decorations. Larger gauges are suitable for canvas work and can be made into three-dimensional shapes.

Canvases for needlepoint

Needlepoint is a type of embroidery worked over a stiff open-weave canvas. Different types of canvas as well as different mesh sizes are available. The mesh or count relates to the number of threads per 2.5cm/1in. Most canvas types are available in white or natural shades.

Single, or mono canvas is a plain-weave canvas that is easily pulled out of shape. For best results, stretch the canvas in a frame, and avoid using diagonal stitches such as tent stitch or half cross stitch.

Interlocking canvas looks similar to single canvas, but the warp threads are twisted around the weft threads during weaving. This renders the fabric fairly stable, making it suitable for all types of canvas embroidery, including diagonal stitches.

Double canvas is woven with pairs of threads rather than single ones. It is used primarily for "tramming", where a thread is laid under the stitches. The sub-divided mesh also makes it easier to work fractional stitches.

Below: 1 Lurex Aida; 2 interlocking canvas; 3 waste canvas; 4 single canvas; 5 Aida; 6 plastic canvas; 7 natural double canvas; 8 coloured even-weave linen; 9 double canvas; 10 Aida; 11 waste canvas; 12 raw linen; 13 single canvas; 14 natural petit point canvas; 15 interlocking canvas; 16 natural single canvas.

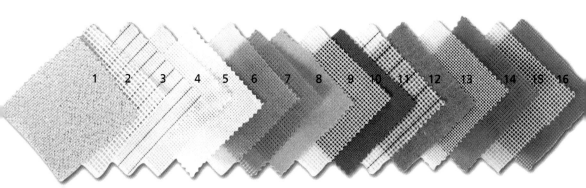

1   2   3   4   5   6   7   8   9   10   11   12   13   14   15   16

Wools (yarns)

Tapestry wool (yarn), crewel wool (yarn) and Persian yarn are the traditional threads used for needlepoint, but almost any thread can be used. Embroidery cottons (floss) such as soft cotton and coton perlé are particularly suitable for 10- or 12-count canvas, and new metallic threads can be stitched easily without fraying or unravelling. Heavier braids can be used on their own, and fine metallic threads and blending filaments can be stitched together with another yarn.

Tapestry wool is a 4-ply, single-strand yarn used on a 10- or 12-count canvas. Use two strands to cover a 7-count canvas with tent stitch. Crewel wool is a 2-ply, single-strand wool. Use three strands to cover a 12-count canvas. Two or three colours of these finer yarns can be blended "in the needle" to produce an interesting effect. Persian yarn consists of three strands of 2-ply yarn. It can be separated to stitch on fine canvas or doubled up for a larger-mesh canvas.

Right: This design makes use of simple stitching and just two colours to convey the impression of a Scandinavian landscape.

Starting and finishing

1 The holes in canvas are quite large, so a knot on the wrong side will work through to the right side. Instead, make a knot on the right side 2.5cm/1in from where you want to stitch. The thread will be secured by your stitches and the knot can be cut off.

2 Whichever wool (yarn) you choose, it must cover the canvas completely, but without being too thick to sew through the canvas. Cut a 45cm/18in length of yarn. A longer length will become thin and frayed before you get to the end.

3 Take the yarn through to the wrong side to finish off. Slide the needle under the stitching for about 2.5cm/1in then trim the thread. Begin new threads in the same way, but avoid running under the same stitches or the work may look uneven.

Counted-thread stitches

These are usually worked over two threads of linen or canvas, or one block of Aida. You can easily alter the scale of the stitches by working over fewer or more threads, changing the thickness of the thread (floss) to suit. The fabric should be covered by the stitch without being cramped and bulky. If you are a beginner, choose a fabric where the holes are symmetrical and easy to see.

Cross stitch

Cross stitch is one of the oldest embroidery stitches. It is worked on canvas or even-weave fabrics so that the stitches are the same size.

Work a row of diagonal stitches in one direction, then cross them with a second row of diagonal stitches slanting in the opposite direction. Make all the top stitches slant in the same direction unless a variation of light and shade is required.

Upright cross stitch

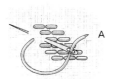
A

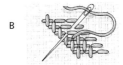
B

Upright cross stitch is a neat stitch suitable for filling small shapes. It looks like a textured woven fabric. To create a different effect, change the spacing between the stitches and the weight of thread (floss) used.

Work rows of evenly spaced horizontal stitches over two threads, diagonally from left to right, until the shape is filled (A). Work vertical stitches over two threads (B). On small shapes, work complete stitches.

Long-armed cross stitch

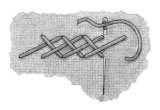

This is a good, textured filling stitch or it can be a border stitch.

Beginning on the left, take a long stitch over eight vertical and four horizontal threads. Bring the needle out four threads down, and cross the stitch with a short stitch over a square of four threads. Bring the needle out four threads down ready to work another stitch. Repeat along the row, making the long stitches twice the length of the short stitches.

Broad cross stitch

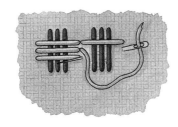

This stitch is used on single canvas to fill large areas. It makes a smooth, textured pattern. Stranded cotton (floss) gives the best coverage.

Work three vertical straight stitches over six threads. Add three horizontal straight stitches of the same length across them. Work the blocks in horizontal rows, fitting subsequent rows of blocks into the spaces in the preceding row.

Half cross stitch

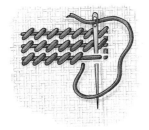

Half cross stitch is stitched on double canvas with "tramming". The stitches are worked over a straight thread sewn between the double canvas threads.

Make a long stitch from right to left, taking the needle between the double threads of the canvas. This padding, or "tramming", helps to cover the canvas. Work diagonal stitches from left to right over the long stitch and the pairs of canvas threads.

Tent stitch

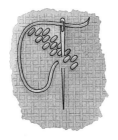

Tent stitch is a small diagonal stitch used mainly on single canvas. The small size of the stitch makes it ideal for working intricate designs from charts or on printed canvas. This stitch is relatively quick to work.

Work across the shape in diagonal rows, as shown, making small half cross stitches over the canvas. Tent stitch can be worked in straight rows but stitching diagonally is less likely to pull the canvas out of shape.

Linen stitch

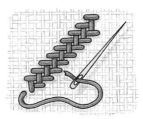

Linen stitch has the appearance of a woven fabric. It is a useful stitch for filling large areas.

Begin at the top right and work a horizontal back stitch over two canvas threads. Work further back stitches diagonally down the canvas, moving one hole behind and down each time. Work vertical stitches over two threads below the horizontal stitches, filling the canvas hole under each one. Repeat to fill the shape.

Brick stitch

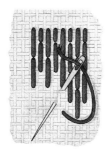

Brick stitch fills a large area quickly and can be worked in different colours for subtle shading. When shading, choose colours that tone so that they merge together.

Work a row of straight stitches, alternately full- and half-length, across the top of the area to be filled. Stagger rows of full-length straight stitches underneath. Fill in the last row with half-length stitches.

Gobelin stitch

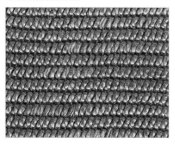

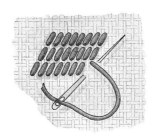

Gobelin stitch can only be worked on single canvas. It produces a flat, ribbed effect. To completely cover the background, use a thick thread.

Beginning on the left, work rows of long diagonal stitches over two horizontal and one vertical canvas thread, inserting the needle upwards each time. Turn around and work back in the opposite direction, this time inserting the needle downwards.

Mosaic stitch

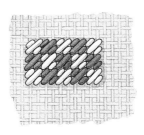

Mosaic stitch is a small, pretty block stitch that fills a nine-hole square. The blocks can be stitched in different colours to create intricate designs. Use a thread with a smooth surface to give the stitch definition. This stitch is quick and easy to do and looks very effective.

Each mosaic has a diagonal stitch that covers three holes, with shorter parallel stitches on each side.

Reverse cushion stitch

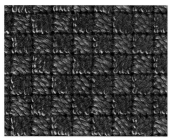

Reverse cushion stitch produces a neat pattern of squares that can be used to fill canvas. The alternating stitch directions give an attractive light-and-shade appearance. For an interesting effect use metallic thread.

Work each reverse cushion stitch block over a square of 16 holes. Work five graduated diagonal straight stitches within the square, starting with a small stitch over two holes. Work the blocks in rows, alternating the direction of the stitches.

Hungarian stitch

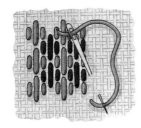

Hungarian stitch can be worked on single or double canvas. It produces a pattern of diamond-shaped blocks.

Hungarian stitch consists of three parallel vertical straight stitches: short ones on each side of a long stitch, worked over two and four horizontal canvas threads. Work the stitch in horizontal rows, leaving two vertical threads between each block. Work subsequent rows in the gaps.

Diamond straight stitch

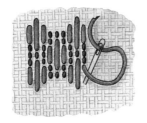

Diamond straight stitch can only be worked on single canvas and can be used to fill a large shape.

Each diamond is made up of five vertical straight stitches worked over one, three or five canvas threads. Work the diamonds so that each row fits neatly into the row above with a single thread space between each one, forming a trellis. Fill in the trellis in a different colour.

Plaited gobelin stitch

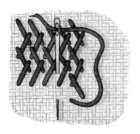

Plaited gobelin stitch produces an attractive interwoven pattern that is quick to work. It will cover a large shape or background if the correct weight of thread (floss) is used.

Beginning at the left, take a stitch over two vertical and one horizontal canvas threads. Stitch with the needle in a vertical position. Work the next row as shown so that the stitches slant in the opposite direction.

Milanese stitch

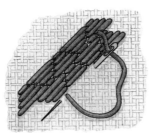

Milanese stitch creates a smooth background that is worked diagonally across the canvas.

Begin at the top right and work a diagonal row of back stitches, making the stitches cover first one then four canvas holes. Work a second row alongside, making the stitches alternately over two and three holes. In the third row make the back stitches alternately over three and two holes. Work row four as row one, beginning with a long stitch.

Knitting stitch

This is a solid filling stitch that looks like knitted stocking stitch.

Work up and down the canvas, beginning at the bottom right. Complete each column in two journeys. Work the right-hand set of stitches slanting upwards over three horizontal canvas threads and across one vertical canvas thread. Work the second set of stitches downwards with a reverse slant.

Star stitch

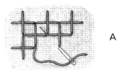

A

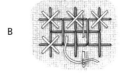

B

Star stitch fills an area with a textured pattern of crosses. It can only be worked on single canvas.

Work upright stitches in horizontal rows, with the four arms of adjacent crosses sharing the same holes in the canvas (A). Overstitch the crosses with two sizes of ordinary cross stitches on alternate rows (B). Work small stitches over two threads and large stitches over four threads.

Rhodes stitch

Rhodes stitch is a decorative filling stitch built up from square blocks.

Work a diagonal straight stitch across five canvas threads from bottom left to top right. Move around the square anti-clockwise (counter-clockwise), working further long diagonal straight stitches until every hole in the square is filled. To make a larger block, work the stitches over six or seven threads, not five.

Half Rhodes stitch

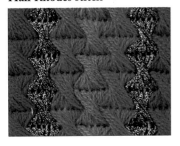

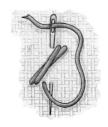

Half Rhodes stitch creates a pattern of bow-tie shapes and makes a stunning textured background or filling when worked in toning colours. This stitch can be worked in any thread on single canvas and is worked over six threads.

Work Rhodes stitch along only the top and bottom sides of the square. Work the next stitch sharing the same holes. Position further columns so that each one interlocks with the preceding one.

Waffle stitch

Waffle stitch consists of a large square block that has a raised diamond in the centre. This stitch is always worked over an odd number of threads. Use a round thread.

Work diagonal stitches following the stitching diagram as your guide. Bring the needle up at 1, down at 2, up at 3 and down at 4, and continue, following the numbers on the diagram until complete.

Rice stitch

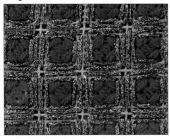

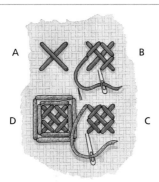

Rice stitch creates an ornate filling stitch when the top layer of crosses is worked in a contrasting thread. The lower layer is usually worked in a thicker thread than the upper layer.

Cover the shape to be filled with a grid of large cross stitches worked over four vertical and four horizontal canvas threads. Work small diagonal stitches across each corner at right angles to make further crosses.

Captive rice stitch

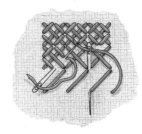

Captive rice stitch is a variation of the stitch with a border around each textured square. Try mixing metallic thread and wool (yarn).

Work a rice stitch over four threads (A and B), then surround it with a double layer of four straight stitches so that it fills a square of six canvas threads (C and D). Fill the small unstitched space between each captive rice stitch with a cross stitch.

Cushion stitch

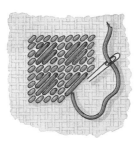

Cushion stitch is a neat, textured, square filling stitch. When worked in two colours it creates a checked pattern known as Scottish stitch. This stitch is most effective when worked in two contrasting threads.

Work blocks of five diagonal stitches over one, three and five canvas thread holes. Slant all the stitches in the same direction and leave a gap of one canvas thread around each square. Work a border of tent stitches around each square.

Chequer stitch

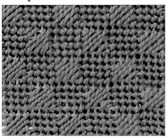

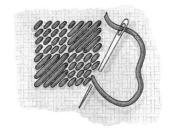

This stitch forms a highly textured square. It is generally worked over a background using one colour, and is best stitched in a shiny thread (floss) such as coton perlé or viscose rayon.

Work blocks of 16 tent stitches to form a chequerboard pattern then fill the spaces in between with seven diagonal straight stitches, as shown. Work all the tent and straight stitches in the same direction.

Ray stitch

Ray stitch makes a pattern like the sun's rays. Work the rows in alternate directions to create a subtle light-and-shade effect. Work this stitch over a four-, six- or eight-hole square and on a loose-weave fabric.

Work seven straight stitches radiating from the bottom right-hand corner of a four-hole canvas square. Pull the stitches tight so that they form a hole at the bottom corner.

Vault stitch

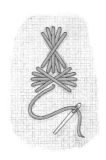

Vault stitches are worked horizontally and vertically in an interlocking grid.

Begin with a vertical vault stitch. Work a straight stitch over eight horizontal threads down the centre. Work a narrow cross stitch of the same length on top, using the holes on each side. Work a wider cross over the top to complete the rectangle. Work alternate horizontal and vertical vault stitches to fill the shape.

Velvet stitch

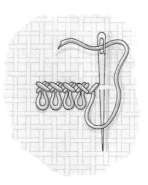

Velvet stitch produces a surface like a long-pile carpet. It looks best worked in wool (yarn) or crewel wool.

Begin at the bottom left-hand corner and work a diagonal back stitch over one canvas thread. Take the needle under the horizontal thread and form a loop, as shown. Work another diagonal stitch across the first one to anchor the loop firmly to the canvas. The long-pile loops can be cut and trimmed to look like velvet once complete.

Scallop stitch

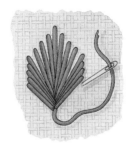

Scallop stitch produces a pattern of interlocking shells that can be used to fill large areas on single canvas.

Work each scallop stitch over eight horizontal and 12 vertical threads. Work a straight stitch over 12 threads down the centre. Work 15 diagonal straight stitches radiating out from the base of the centre stitch, as shown. Arrange the shell shapes in horizontal rows and interlock subsequent rows.

Fan stitch

Fan stitch forms an intricate pattern that fills large areas of single canvas.

Work the fan over five vertical and ten horizontal threads. Work 15 straight stitches of different lengths, all radiating from the same central hole. Below the fan, work five stitches spanning four horizontal threads and three vertical canvas threads. Below, work a vertical straight stitch over two threads.

Fir (Pine) stitch

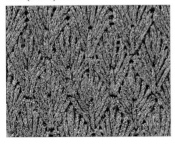

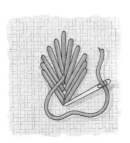

Fir (pine) stitch can be worked individually or as an ornate filling on single canvas. Shade the motifs by using several tones of one colour.

Work a central vertical straight stitch over six threads. Work five diagonal stitches of varying lengths to the left and right, using the five canvas holes below the vertical stitch. To finish, work a vertical stitch over these five holes.

Eyelets

Eyelets makes an attractive diamond that can be turned on its side to make a square, or can be modified to become a circle.

Work each diamond in a block over ten canvas threads. Stitch 18 satin stitches of graduated length, radiating from the same hole in the centre. Frame the block with back stitches. Work each circular eyelet in a block of six canvas threads. Work 16 satin stitches, radiating from the same hole in the centre.

Assisi embroidery

Assisi embroidery is a type of cross stitch originating from Assisi in Italy. For this, the normal principles of cross stitch are reversed so that the design area is left blank and the background filled in with rows of cross stitches. Traditional Assisi designs are heraldic and often feature real or mythical birds, animals and flowers. Assisi embroidery is sewn in a combination of blue, red or black threads (floss) on white or cream linen.

Holbein stitch

An essential feature of Assisi embroidery is the Holbein stitch used to outline the cross stitch, and to create the pretty filigree border that is typical of this style of embroidery. Before working any cross stitches, outline the design area with Holbein stitch (see Blackwork).

Above and below: Both examples have been worked in the Assisi style, but the example below does not have the traditional Holbein stitch outline.

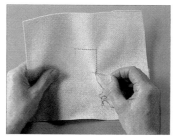

1 Work a row of running stitches around the outside edge of the cross stitch area.

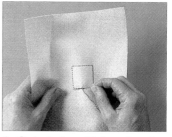

2 Go back along this line of running stitch, filling in the gaps between the stitches on the return journey.

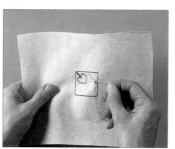

3 Outline the motifs in Holbein stitch in the same way, then fill in the background with cross stitch.

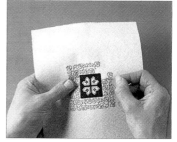

4 Work the details and filigree border in very fine gold braid.

Blackwork

As its name implies, blackwork is worked with black thread (floss). It probably originated among the Muslim communities of the Middle East, where the teachings of the Koran forbade the use of figurative designs. The Moors brought the technique to Europe during their 700-year occupation of Spain. It is thought that Catherine of Aragon made it popular in Britain at the beginning of the sixteenth century.

Blackwork features on many of the garments shown in English court paintings from around the time of King Henry VIII. It is thought that the fashion for blackwork began with the arrival of his wife, Catherine of Aragon, from Spain. One artist in particular, the younger Hans Holbein, painted the ornate blackwork collars and cuffs with such exquisite detail that his name became synonymous with one of the stitches used.

During the Elizabethan era, blackwork was greatly influenced by Jacobean crewel embroidery. Around this time gold began to be used on the designs, and they became increasingly extravagant, featuring coiled goldwork stems and beautiful blackwork flowers.

Blackwork is traditionally worked in silk on fine linen but it can also be worked on Aida using stranded cotton, with the delicate blackwork patterns formed using a single strand of thread (floss). Use a heavier thread such as coton à broder or coton perlé to outline the design. Use fine metallic thread or very fine gold braid for any goldwork details.

How to stitch blackwork

Blackwork patterns are worked in two straight stitches: back stitch and Holbein stitch. Use back stitch for broken lines in the pattern and Holbein stitch for continuous lines. Find the shortest route along the design lines so that you can keep stitching for as long as possible with one strand of thread.

Holbein stitch consists of a double row of running stitches. Work a row of running stitches along the design lines (on linen work each stitch over two threads), leaving a gap the same size as the stitches in between. Then work back filling in the gaps with a second row of running stitches. To prevent the line from looking crenellated, bring the thread out above one running stitch and insert the needle below the next one.

Creating a blackwork pattern

Blackwork patterns are fascinating to stitch and amazingly easy to design. Exquisite geometric designs can be constructed from simple patterns that are repeated in a linear or symmetrical format. Use graph paper or a basic graphics computer program to produce suitable designs.

A good way to keep a record of patterns for future reference is by stitching them on a sampler. Mark a piece of linen into 4cm/1½in squares and stitch a different pattern in each one. The squares in the sampler overleaf are graded from dark at the top to light at the bottom. This makes it easy to select suitable patterns for designs.

Below: Blackwork is ideal for representational pieces, where the stitch density effectively creates areas of light and shade.

Making a blackwork picture

The most effective blackwork pictures are simple in design and have distinctive bold shapes filled with different stitch patterns.

Blackwork patterns are by nature light, medium or dark. The density of the stitches determines the depth of light or shade in the pattern. You can easily adapt patterns to make them darker or lighter by adding or removing some of the lines. Blackwork patterns can be used to create a three-dimensional effect. Choose darker patterns to make parts of the design appear farther away and lighter patterns for the foreground. Plan your design carefully before beginning to stitch.

1 Draw out the design in pencil. Decide which parts of the design will be light, medium or dark. The lightest areas will seem further forward than the dark areas. Cross-hatch sections of the design to build up the density of shading required. Erase or darken areas until you have found a pleasing balance.

2 Draw along the lines of the design in black felt pen and trace directly through on to the fabric with a soft pencil. Choose blackwork patterns that will fit the different light, medium and dark areas of the design. Try out the different patterns on graph paper to check the density of colour before beginning to stitch.

Above: Use the template provided at the back of the book as your design source, then fill in the areas using some of the blackwork designs pictured on the right.

3 Work the blackwork patterns in Holbein stitch or back stitch, using a single strand of black stranded cotton (floss). Work the patterns carefully, filling the shapes accurately.

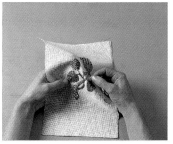

4 Embroider a line of stem stitches along all the design lines using a heavy black thread such as coton à broder. Press on the wrong side.

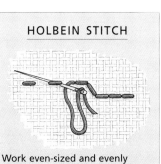

HOLBEIN STITCH

Work even-sized and evenly spaced running stitches along the design lines. Then work back, filling in the gaps with a second row of running stitches.

Right: These are just a selection of the hundreds of patterns that can be created in blackwork. Practise making the stitches neat and even, then develop your own designs either on graph paper or using a computer graphics program.

Hardanger embroidery

This form of cutwork originates from the town of Hardanger in Norway. It consists of blocks of satin stitches known as "kloster" blocks formed into a geometric outline. The fabric inside the blocks is carefully cut away, except for a few thread bars which divide the space up into additional squares. These thread bars are used to decorate the space with delicate needlelace and weaving.

Making a kloster block

A kloster block consists of five satin stitches worked over four fabric threads. The area around the kloster blocks is usually filled with surface embroidery in a geometric pattern, worked in satin stitch and other simple stitches such as chain stitch.

Hardanger embroidery is traditionally worked on a heavy even-weave linen or on 22-count special Hardanger fabric. Use thread (floss) that is slightly heavier than the weave of the linen. A round thread such as coton à broder gives the best effect for Hardanger. Precise stitching is the key to this technique.

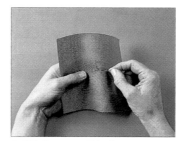

1 Work two small back stitches, leaving a tail of thread (this will be sewn in later). Stitch the first block of five satin stitches, then take a large diagonal stitch, bringing the needle out four threads to the left of where the thread last emerged.

2 To work blocks on the diagonal, stitch one kloster block, but take a back stitch on the last satin stitch. This will bring the needle out at the corner of the kloster block ready to begin the horizontal satin stitches of the next block.

Completing the cutwork

Baste the shape you wish to create on to the fabric before you work the kloster blocks and use this as a guideline. If the threads inside the blocks are to be cut, make sure the blocks are positioned directly opposite each other. Once complete, run the thread under a kloster block on the wrong side to secure it and trim. Unpick the back stitches and sew this thread in on the wrong side too.

1 Using sharp scissors, cut four fabric threads along the edge of a block. Cut the same four threads at the other side and pull the threads out one at a time with tweezers. Cut the horizontal threads in the same way.

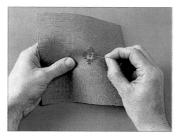

2 Leave the threads in the centre where there are no kloster blocks. These bars left inside the cutwork are covered decoratively. The simplest way to cover them is with closely worked overcasting stitches.

3 The thread bars can be woven or wrapped. Secure the thread on the wrong side and weave under and over two fabric threads until the bar is full. Move to the next bar by weaving through the blocks on the wrong side.

Adding the decorative filling

The following stitch diagrams show just a few of the stitching techniques used to decorate kloster blocks.

Work a small sampler of kloster blocks, then practise filling the areas with the designs here. Leave some blank and fill others with the lacy designs. As you reach the end of each thread (floss), weave it in under and over the fabric and stitching threads on the wrong side of the work.

Above: Detail of a garment showing wrapped, woven and picot bars.

Above: Geometric surface embroidery has been used here to decorate areas of fabric in between Hardanger embroidery.

Wrapped bars

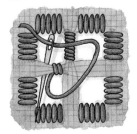

Overcast the thread bars tightly. Sew the thread end in securely on the wrong side by weaving it in and out of the newly created bars.

Picot

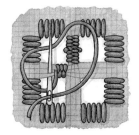

Picots are small decorative knots that are worked half-way down a woven bar. Insert the needle as shown and wrap the working thread around before pulling it through.

Lace stitch

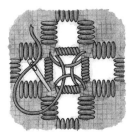

Insertion stitches are used to fill the spaces in Hardanger embroidery. Take a stitch in each corner interlacing the threads.

Woven bars

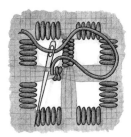

Weave under and over two threads to make a solid bar. Take the thread under the stitches on the wrong side ready to begin the next bar.

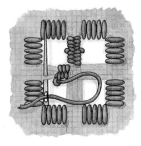

Weave under and over two threads, then make another picot on the other side. Complete the bar, then stitch under the blocks on the wrong side to begin the next bar.

Twisted lace filling stitch

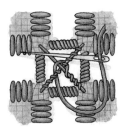

Work a cross stitch across the space and wrap loosely. This insertion stitch produces a star in the centre if worked across the wrapped or woven bars.

Pulled-fabric embroidery

Pulled fabric, also known as punchwork, is a type of counted-thread embroidery that creates attractive lacy patterns on the fabric. The weave of the fabric used and how tightly the stitches are pulled will determine how pronounced the holes in your design will be. Pulled-fabric work began as peasant embroidery, and later developed into an exquisitely fine embroidery, requiring high standards of workmanship.

Pulled-fabric embroidery is more prominent on an even-weave linen, whereas a scrim or muslin fabric is so easily pulled that the shape and pattern of the holes come to the fore. It is traditionally worked in a thread (floss) that matches the fabric colour so that the lace effect is seen. Stretch the fabric in a hoop for best effect.

Left: This balustrade has pulled fabric worked in some areas of the design.

There are several types of pulled-fabric stitches. Diagonal stitches create a lacy effect. Isolated stitches can also be grouped together to form a filling. Surface stitches, such as coll filling stitch, are worked with different groupings of satin stitches. This group of stitches are not pulled as tightly as other pulled-thread stitches and so the embroidery is more prominent than the holes.

Punch stitch

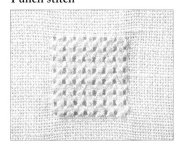

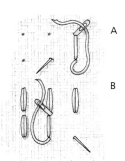

A

B

Punch stitch is one of the most common pulled-thread stitches and is often worked on its own. It is a square stitch worked in two steps.

Work rows of double straight stitches four threads apart following the illustration as a guide (A and B), then complete the square pattern with pairs of horizontal straight stitches. Punch stitch will form large holes if the stitches are pulled tight and if the fabric has a very loose weave.

Wave stitch

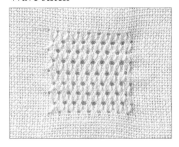

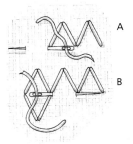

A

B

Wave stitch makes a trellis pattern similar to brickwork. Pull the threads tightly to make large holes.

Work from right to left and back again across two threads and down four threads, always inserting the needle in a horizontal position (A). To begin another row, bring the needle down over eight threads and then turn the work upside down to stitch in the same way as before (B).

Coll filling stitch

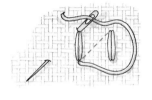

Coll filling is a surface stitch worked in rows from right to left. The threads are not pulled as tightly in this stitch, making more of the embroidery stitch than the lacy or holey patterns.

Work three satin stitches vertically over four fabric threads. Space the groups of satin stitches in the second row between the previous stitches to form a brick-like arrangement.

Oblique filling

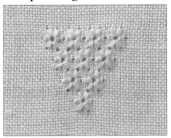

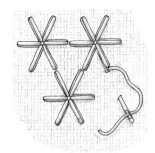

Oblique filling can create quite large holes in a loose-weave fabric if it is pulled tight. It can be worked as individual star-shaped eyelets, or together as a filling stitch. Experiment with different threads (floss).

Fill a block of eight fabric threads with six double stitches as shown. Make each stitch go through the same central hole. Use the same outside holes for adjoining stars.

Three-sided stitch

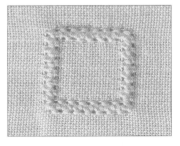

A

B

C

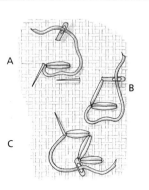

This stitch can be worked in rows as a filling but is often worked as a border. The stitches can be worked to form an attractive curved corner.

Work three-sided stitch from right to left, turning the fabric around to work in a different direction (A–C). The stitch is made up of three pairs of back stitches, worked in a block of four threads. Work the stitch as a border, in rows or in a solid block, with the next row sharing the same holes as the previous one.

Eyelets

Eyelets can be worked individually, in rows or as a grid pattern. The stitches can be made a different size, provided all the stitches go into the same central square and are spaced evenly around the sides.

A small eyelet is worked over a block of four fabric threads. Use a strong thread that will not snap when it is pulled tight to form a large centre hole.

Drawn-thread work

Several types of embroidery are included under the heading drawn-thread work. It is often confused with pulled-fabric embroidery, but is a totally different technique. Fabric threads are withdrawn: the remaining weft or warp threads are then embroidered to create delicate lace patterns. Drawn-thread work is used today to decorate plain table linen or to add delicate embroidery to a christening gown.

Withdrawing threads

1 Using a small, sharp pair of embroidery scissors, insert the tip of the scissors between two vertical fabric threads and cut across ten horizontal fabric threads. Use a tapestry needle to ease the horizontal threads out one at a time.

2 If the threads are not pulled out completely, the ends must be finished off neatly. Pull out all the horizontal threads up to the same vertical thread. Turn the fabric over and darn each thread in for about 1cm/¹⁄₂in.

3 You can also finish the ends off with buttonhole stitches. Work the buttonhole stitch over four or five threads along the edge of the channel. Trim the threads close to the stitching.

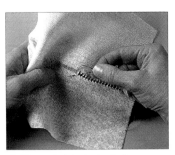

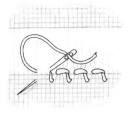

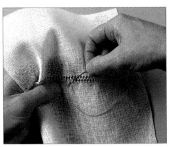

4 Hem stitch is the basic drawn-thread stitch. It is used to group the threads into bundles and finish the edge. It can also be used to hold a hem in position on the wrong side.

5 Work along one side from right to left, grouping the threads into bundles of four.

6 Work hem stitch along the other edge. The threads can either form bars, or the bundles can be split in two to make a zigzag pattern.

Right, from left to right: double or Italian hem stitch, chevron stitch border, zigzag, twisted bars, straight bars, tied bars, double twists.

Working with wider drawn-thread bands

1 Pull out 20 threads and make a wide ladder border. Secure the thread (floss) at one end. Work a buttonhole stitch to hold it in the middle of the bars. Lift the second bar back over the first, using the needle. Pull the needle through under the first bar.

2 Different patterns can be worked by twisting the bars in groups of two, or in double rows as shown. You will need a wider band, between 25 and 30 drawn threads, to accommodate the extra row of twists.

3 Embroidery stitches can be used to tie the bars together. Twisted chain stitch or coral stitch are commonly used. Secure the embroidery thread at the end of the bar and work from the right side, pulling the stitches tight.

4 Some stitches can also be used in place of hem stitch. Choose stitches that naturally pull the threads together in bundles. Both stem stitch and chevron stitch are suitable.

5 Strengthen wide borders by leaving a narrow band of unpulled threads between the rows. The outside edges are finished with hem stitch but the inner edges can be embroidered.

Above: This gown was made from fine cotton lawn and embroidered with silk. Drawn-thread work features on the bodice.

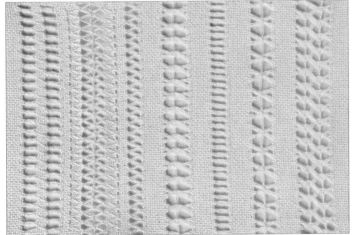

Russian drawn-thread embroidery

As its name implies, this technique originated in Russia. It is an exquisite fine embroidery that is very easy to work. Unlike other types of drawn-thread work, it is worked in blocks rather than rows and the open grid forms the background for simple motifs. The design is marked on the linen first and the border outlined in buttonhole stitch. The solid motifs are traditionally outlined with heavy chain stitches.

Getting started

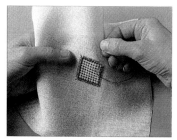

1 Mark the outer edge of the drawn-thread work with basting, ensuring that the square has an even number of threads in each direction. Cut the threads in pairs. Cut a pair of horizontal threads, then leave the next two threads uncut between two vertical threads. Turn and cut every second pair of vertical threads.

2 Trim the drawn threads close to the fabric and work buttonhole stitches neatly around the edges of the square. Stitch through every second thread to avoid bunching the stitches. Use a magnifying lamp to work the buttonhole stitch and overcasting so that you can see exactly where to stitch.

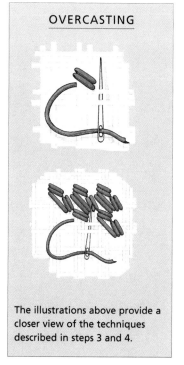

OVERCASTING

The illustrations above provide a closer view of the techniques described in steps 3 and 4.

Below: Russian drawn-thread work is often used to decorate table linen.

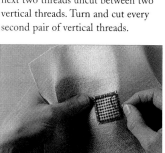

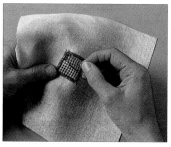

3 Beginning at the first pair of threads on the top edge, work two overcasting stitches over the thread bars. Work a stitch across the corner and then another two on the next bar.

4 Feed the embroidery thread (floss) down to the next bar along the buttonhole stitches on the wrong side. Continue overcasting the bars in diagonal rows until the grid is covered.

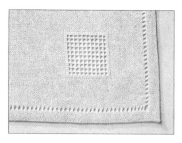

Needle weaving

This is a type of drawn-thread embroidery worked in narrow borders. Needle-woven borders are stronger than hem-stitched drawn-thread work because the fabric threads are densely covered with embroidery threads (floss). Needle weaving is normally worked with coloured threads and can be used in conjunction with other embroidery techniques such as Hardanger.

STARTING AND FINISHING

Begin as for drawn-thread work by pulling out enough weft threads to form a wide band.

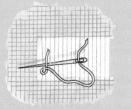

• Hold a long loop of thread (floss) down the thread bars and work wrapping or weaving stitches over the top to secure it.

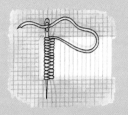

• Sew the end of the thread down inside the bar and snip off the end to finish.

• Finish the ends of the band with buttonhole stitches or by sewing them in. Hem stitch the top and bottom edges as desired.

Ladder pattern

Overcast groups of threads to create a ladder pattern, or weave groups of threads together. These bars have been decorated with picots.

Woven bars

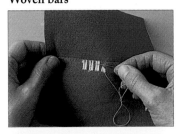

1 Begin in the centre between the groups of threads and weave from side to side until the bars are filled with stitches.

Zigzag pattern

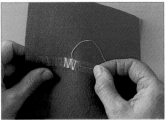

Make a zigzag pattern by wrapping the completed bar with the next group of threads.

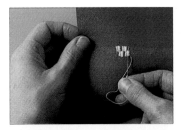

2 Woven bars can be split to create a number of "brickwork" patterns. Feed the needle up through the woven bars to reach the next starting point.

Broderie anglaise

This technique falls into the category of "whitework", a term that encompasses a number of techniques such as pulled-thread embroidery, drawn thread, Mountmellick and Casalguidi. All are traditionally worked using white thread (floss) on white fabric.

Broderie anglaise

Broderie anglaise is exquisite lacy embroidery combining fine surface stitches with eyelets of different sizes and shapes. The holes in the fabric are cut or punched with a round tool, such as a stiletto, and then overcast.

It was most popular at the end of the eighteenth century when caps, clothes and fine household linen were decorated with elaborate patterns.

Broderie anglaise is traditionally finished with a scalloped edge. The designs are usually formed from an arrangement of simple floral motifs. Mark the design on a closely woven fine cotton or linen.

Eyelets

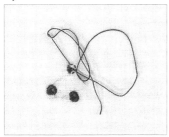

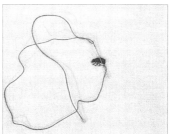

1 To make eyelets, work a row of tiny running stitches in a small circle, less than 5mm/¼in in diameter. Punch small eyelets with a stiletto or the point of fine embroidery scissors in the centre of the stitches. Work overcasting stitches around the edge and sew the thread (floss) end in.

2 Outline larger holes with running stitches as before, then cut across the centre of the hole both horizontally and vertically. Turn the fabric flap to the wrong side and overcast the edge. Trim any excess fabric from the wrong side. Larger oval eyelets are surrounded by padded satin stitches.

Scallops

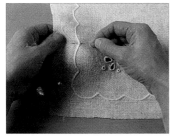

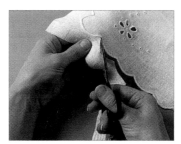

1 Outline the area with chain stitch as padding. Stitch closely worked buttonhole stitch over the top.

2 Trim very close to the stitching with small, sharp scissors.

Needlelace

This type of lace-making is most often associated with stumpwork, a style of embroidery that was popular in seventeenth-century Britain. It is used to cover padded appliqué shapes and can be worked over wire to create three-dimensional petals and flowers. The delicacy and beauty of needlelace lies in the evenness and regularity of the stitches, so it must be worked on a firm foundation of threads (floss) or wire.

Needlelace can be worked across a couched thread (floss) shape to give a firm foundation to the stitches. In stumpwork this is known as a "cordonnet". The cordonnet and needlelace are worked over a piece of PVC or other firm fabric so that they can be made to the exact shape required. Once complete, the cordonnet and needlelace are lifted off the temporary backing and stitched in place on the embroidery.

Right: Stumpwork birds with wired wings are clothed in needlelace. The needlelace shoreline sits on a space-dyed background of calico and scrim.

MAKING A CORDONNET

• Trace the required shape on to paper and cut out. Position the shape on top of a piece of calico. Cut a piece of PVC larger than your shape, place it on top of the calico and baste.

• Pin prick around the line to transfer the shape to the PVC. If the shape will be padded, pin prick slightly outside the line.

• Fold a length of strong thread (floss) in half and catch the loop end down on the marked line. Use thread in the colour that you

will be working with. If the shape is to stand away from the fabric, for example, for a petal, add a piece of fine wire on top of the thread, leaving a wire stalk. This can be cut off later.

• Couch the double thread and wire down around the outline. Work the stitches closer together on tight curves and work two stitches in corners to make a sharp point. Slip the ends of the couched threads through the loop. Trim the ends to 1cm/½in and bend one end back on itself.

• Overcast the ends over the cordonnet only, to secure.

• Work the needlelace over the cordonnet, without stitching through the PVC.

Getting started

Needlelace stitches are nearly all based on a simple loop or blanket stitch. Different patterns are created by stitching different numbers of stitches into loops and leaving spaces in between others. This technique is intended to be finely worked: historically lacemakers would stitch hundreds of tiny stitches to the square 2.5cm/1in! There are many hundreds of needlelace stitches to choose from. Just a few of the more common ones are listed here.

Starting a new thread (floss)

You will probably need more than one length of thread (floss) to work a panel of needlelace. Don't use a piece longer than 45–50cm/18–20in in your tapestry needle otherwise it is likely to get tangled and become knotted as

you work, or if you are using fine silk thread it will unravel. As a rule, it is safe to continue working if your thread is about twice the length of the row you are about to start. If it is less, you will need to start a new thread. Wrap the old thread around the cordonnet and leave a short end lying around the shape outline. Introduce the new thread by wrapping it twice around the outline to secure it in place. The ends are held in place by buttonhole stitches at the end.

Increasing and decreasing

Increase or decrease the number of stitches at the end of a row. To increase, work extra stitches into the last loop. Then make sure you begin in the right loop to keep the pattern correct when you are working back

along the row. To decrease, miss the first loop and work along the row to the last loop. Then wrap the thread around the side of the cordonnet and continue as before.

Finishing

Once complete, twist any wire ends together and remove the excess. Work tightly packed buttonhole stitches around the edge of the needlelace, stitching under the cordonnet but not through the PVC.

From the wrong side (the calico side), clip the couching threads. Carefully lift the needlelace off the PVC. Use tweezers to remove any couching thread ends. Slip stitch the piece to the background as invisibly as possible. Mould the wire into shape at this point if required.

Bruxelles stitch

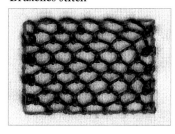

Bruxelles (Brussels) stitch is one of the most versatile needlelace stitches because it can be worked in pairs or trebles, and can be whipped or corded.

Wrap the thread twice around one side of the cordonnet and work even blanket stitch along the top of the cordonnet. Wrap the thread around the cordonnet at the other end before continuing back along the last row of loops. Keep the same number of stitches in each row by missing the last loop.

Double Bruxelles stitch

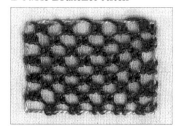

Work two blanket stitches along the top edge of the cordonnet, then leave a space equal to two stitches before working another pair of blanket stitches. Continue across the row until you reach the other side. Wrap the thread around the side of the cordonnet and then work back across the row in the same way. Continue to fill the shape.

Whipped treble Bruxelles stitch

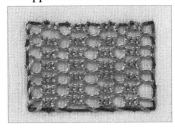

Work groups of three blanket stitches along the top of the cordonnet, leaving a space equal to two stitches between them. Work across the row. Wrap the thread (floss) around the side cordonnet. Whip the thread back over each loop (including the last one). Wrap around the cordonnet, then work blanket stitches into each loop and continue as before.

Point d'Anvers

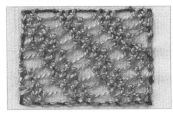

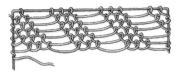

Work three blanket stitches along the top edge of the cordonnet, then leave a space equal to three stitches and work another three. Wrap the thread around the side of the cordonnet. Work back across the row, making one stitch into the long loop and two more into the loops between the three stitches above.

Pea stitch variation

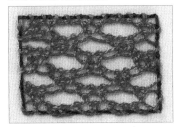

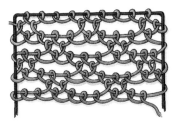

Work blanket stitches across the top of the cordonnet. Wrap the thread around the cordonnet side, then work two blanket stitches into the first two loops. Miss two loops and work blanket stitch into the next two until the row end. Wrap the thread around the cordonnet. Work one stitch into the small loop between two stitches and three into the long loop. At the end of the row, wrap the thread twice around the cordonnet and complete the pattern.

Corded Bruxelles stitch

This is a more stable, denser variation of Bruxelles stitch. It can be adapted for double and treble Bruxelles stitch.

Work a row of blanket stitches as for Bruxelles stitch. Wrap the thread around the side cordonnet and take it straight back across to the other side without making any stitches. Wrap the thread around the side cordonnet twice and then work a row of blanket stitches into each loop, catching the straight thread.

Goldwork

Today, goldwork is a generic term that covers all types of metallic thread embroidery. Traditional threads (floss) such as Japan gold, Russian braid and gold cord have a proportion of real gold in them which creates a wonderful effect when the light catches different facets of the thread.

Materials

There is a wonderful selection of exquisite metallic and silk threads (floss) to choose from.

1 Japan gold

Japan gold was traditionally made from fine ribbons of real gold coiled around silk floss. Today gold or silver lurex threads are wrapped around a thread core. Japan gold must be couched on to fabric because the metal layer will rip if stitched.

2 Braids and cords

There are many different heavy metallic threads that can be couched on to fabric. These provide a wide range of textures. They are available in many colours.

3 Metallic threads (floss)

Some metallic threads can be stitched by hand and some can even be used in a sewing machine. To test a thread's flexibility, run your nails down it. If this makes it unravel, it is only suitable for couching.

4 Purl

Purl is made from fine wire that is coiled to form a tiny spring. It is made in a continuous length that can be cut to size and stitched like a bead. Rough purl has a soft polished finish and smooth purl is highly polished and shiny. Check purl has a sparkly appearance because the wire spring is kinked. Pearl or wire purl is heavier in weight and is usually pulled out and couched on to fabric.

5 Gold kid

These are shiny metallic pieces of leather which can be cut up and applied to goldwork. Keep the pieces small and work stitches over the top to blend them into the design. Imitation kid has a synthetic backing.

6 Felt

Felt is used as a padding for gold kid and purl. Use yellow felt with gold threads and grey with silver. Make graded shapes to build up a thick pad, with the largest shape on top.

7 Silk threads

Use silk thread for couching gold threads. It has a wonderful sheen and is strong and elastic. Use a yellow colour with gold threads and grey with silver.

THREADS (FLOSS)

- The first metallic threads (floss) were made in such a way that it was physically impossible to stitch them through fabric.

- New synthetic metallic threads have recently been developed that can be stitched in the same way as any other embroidery thread. They are easy to use and do not tarnish, but give a uniform sparkle that unfortunately has none of the softness or warmth of real gold.

- It is essential to buy good-quality gold thread because the cheaper imitations will quickly tarnish. The same applies to the fabric that the work is stitched on and all other embroidery threads used in the design.

- Natural threads and fabrics such as cotton or linen can be used, but silk is without question the most suitable fibre. Its aptness lies not only in its wonderful sheen, but also in the strength and elasticity of the thread and the rich colours that offset gold so well.

- Most metallic threads are simply laid over the fabric and couched down. The couched threads can be almost invisible or can play a big part in the design.

Couching

In the Middle Ages underside couching was devised as a method to secure rigid gold threads (floss) to a background fabric. This method of couching, where stitching is worked from the wrong side of the fabric and the laid threads pulled to the back, is now obsolete. However, couching (from the right side) remains the principal method of attaching thick cords or threads.

To begin, stretch the fabric in an embroidery hoop or frame and run a length of silk thread over a piece of beeswax. This helps to prevent the couching thread from twisting as you stitch. Cut a length of gold thread (to be couched) and tape the ends to prevent them from unravelling.

1 Pin the length of gold thread along the design line, leaving a 2.5cm/1in tail. Bring the silk thread up next to the gold thread and make a straight stitch at right angles across the thread. Work further straight stitches 5mm/¼in apart. Thin gold threads are usually couched in pairs so that they lie closer together.

2 Leave about 2.5cm/1in at the end of the row. Use a large-eyed embroidery needle to take the embroidery thread through to the wrong side. It is better to make a large hole that will be covered by the gold thread than to snag or tear the fabric by forcing the thread through with too small a needle.

Using string

Use string to make raised areas of goldwork. The string can be of varying thickness and the spacing altered to create different effects. If possible, use a string to match the metallic thread. String can be dyed if a good match is difficult to find.

1 Cut lengths of string the same size and stitch down in parallel rows on the fabric. Leave a gap between each row. Work double oversewing stitches at each end and catch the string down on long lengths.

2 Couch the gold threads over the string, working double stitches at each side. Take the ends of the thread to the wrong side as before. A basket-weave pattern can be created by couching over alternate pairs of string.

Right: The skill in goldwork lies in the careful manipulation of the exquisite threads (floss). It takes time and effort to create a successful goldwork design. While it is good to be innovative, don't be tempted to distort and mangle the metallic threads in an attempt to be original.

Far right: Goldwork can be enhanced by other embroidery stitches such as bullion knots. These are the same shape as cut purl and look very effective.

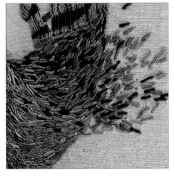

COUCHING A PATTERN OR SHAPE

CREATING PATTERNS

Metal threads (floss) can be couched in different patterns by working stitches between the previous stitches or by stepping to one side. See below.

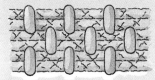

BRICKWORK

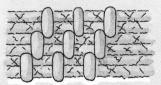

STEPPING

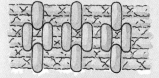

REPEAT PATTERN

CIRCLES

• To make circles, fold in half a long length of gold thread.

• Couch the folded end at the centre of the circle.

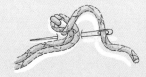

• Coil the double thread around, couching at right angles to the gold thread.

• When sewing in the thread ends, stagger them to make a smooth outline.

ANGLED SHAPES

Outline pointed shapes with a double length of gold thread. For a very sharp point, work one thread over each gold thread.

• Couch pairs of gold threads down each side of the shape, leaving a 2.5cm/1in tail of thread at the point. Continue couching pairs of threads down each side, alternately until the shape has been filled.

• Once complete, take the gold threads through to the wrong side and tie off.

Above and right: Use fine thread (floss) to create couched patterns.

Purl

Purl is a long metallic spring produced specially for goldwork. It can be cut up and stitched like beads or couched down like a gold thread (floss). Purl is pliable and can be cut into lengths up to 1cm/¹/₂in when stitched over padding. There are several types of purl, such as check and smooth, which reflect the light to give different effects.

Purl looks very effective when stitched randomly on padded felt. When it is cut in short lengths, it can also be used as a powdering over the background of the design.

1 Use a small pair of craft scissors to cut purl because the wire will quickly blunt embroidery scissors. Cut it at right angles with a quick, clean cut. Let the purl fall into a small dish to keep it safe.

2 Using a strong thread or a double length of silk thread (floss), pick up the purl with the needle point. Take the needle to the wrong side. The purl can be stitched to lie flat or worked over other pieces of purl or string.

Padding

One of the main characteristics of goldwork is the attractive play of light on the different threads. To increase this effect, areas can be padded and covered with gold threads, kid or purl. You can use string or card (card stock) as a padding material, but felt is the most common choice. Match the colour of the padding to the thread colour – yellow for gold and grey for silver.

1 Decide on the shape and size of the padded area. Cut a felt shape that size then cut two or three smaller pieces to fit underneath.

Attaching kid

1 Cut the kid to the required shape. Hold it in place with your thumb. Bring the thread up next to the shape and stab stitch through to the wrong side. Work around the shape, stab stitching every 5mm/¹/₄in.

2 Place the smallest piece in the middle of the shape and catch it down with stab stitches. Attach the other layers in this way.

3 Sew the purl, kid or gold threads on top, stitching into the felt in the middle and through all the layers at the edge.

Right: This goldwork design uses a variety of techniques. The delicate wadding (batting) is a soft contrast to the gold thread (floss) and kid leather.

Beadwork

Beads conjure up images of exquisite, heavily encrusted evening wear and beautiful accessories such as bags or slippers. But beads can also be used to add detail and texture to other embroidery techniques such as cross stitch, canvas work, appliqué and freestyle embroidery.

Beads come in all shapes and sizes and can be stitched individually or couched in rows. Whatever their size, the technique for stitching them is basically the same. No special equipment is required, although seed beads and thin bugle beads have such tiny holes that a special beading needle may be needed.

Beading needles are exceptionally long and fine and are ideal for threading large numbers of beads for couching. It is usually possible to use a fine ordinary "between" needle for all but the tiniest beads. You will probably find the shorter length of this type of needle easy to handle. If a bead gets stuck on the needle partway down, do not force it over the eye. If you cannot get it back off the needle, crush the bead with small parallel pliers and choose another.

Getting started

Use a double thread (floss) for sewing beads if possible. Fold a long length in half and thread the cut ends into the needle. Bring the needle up through the fabric, leaving a thread loop underneath. Take the needle back down through the fabric and the loop, then pull tight to secure. This is a very secure way to begin sewing. If a single strand is used, begin with a knot and stitch back through the knot for extra security. Tip a few beads into a small flat dish that has a rim ready to start. It is easier to pick the beads up with the point of the needle against the edge of the dish.

Couching

1 Couching is a quick and neat way to attach a long row of beads. You can also see at a glance what the line will look like before sewing the beads in place. Any beads that lie together well can be used. Thread two needles for couching. Secure the first double length at the beginning of the line to be covered. Thread on the beads in the required order.

2 Bring the second threaded needle up between the first two beads. Take the thread (floss) over the string of beads and back down on the other side. Sew a couching stitch between every bead. At the end of the line, remove any excess beads. Take all the threads through to the wrong side and sew in the ends securely.

Above: Carefully selected beads add subtle interest to the design of this hand- and machine-embroidered fan.

Making a bead net

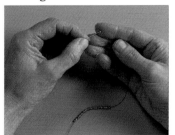

1 Thread a fine needle with a long length of waxed thread (floss). For row 1, thread on an odd number of beads: 25 is a good number. Let the beads lie on the tabletop so that they do not fall off the end of the thread.

2 To make the second row, add two beads and take the needle back through the fourth bead (the second bead on row 1). Carry on adding two beads and catching the fourth until you reach the end.

3 On the next row add two beads between the previous pairs.

4 Keep adding rows in this way until the netted fabric forms.

Above: This stunning smocked purse is decorated with a bead net and tassels.

Attaching single beads

Bring the thread up to the right side of the fabric and pick up a bead. Let the bead drop down to the end of the thread and sew back through the fabric at the end of the bead.

Attaching bugle beads

Bugle beads are sewn in the same way as small beads. Thread a bugle bead and stitch back down where the other end will lie. Hold the first bead in place with your thumb to get the length right. Take the thread across the back to the left-hand side and attach as before.

Attaching sequins

Sequins can be attached with a small bead. Bring the thread up through the fabric and thread on first a sequin then a small bead. Take the needle back through the hole in the sequin and the small bead will hide this.

Hand-stitched appliqué

Appliqué takes its name from the French verb "appliquer" meaning "to apply". The technique involves cutting fabric to shape and sewing it on to a background fabric. Appliqué has evolved into a highly decorative art and is used in various forms all over the world. The people of Hawaii and Laos, for example, stitch intricate forms of reverse appliqué, and in North America wonderful pictorial appliqué is sewn.

Raw-edge appliqué

Use this method for non-fray fabrics such as felt, or to give a ragged look to raw edges. Iron lightweight interfacing to the wrong side of woven fabrics before cutting out, or iron the appliqué to the main fabric with fusible bonding web.

Felt appliqué looks particularly effective if blanket stitch or another embroidery stitch is worked around the edge of each piece.

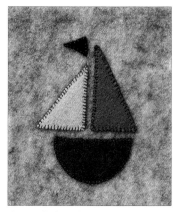

Above: Felt always has a neat, trimmed raw edge that does not fray. For this reason it is a good choice for beginners.

Alternatively, you may choose to make a feature of frayed raw edges, choosing fabrics such as scrim or other loosely woven fabrics that fray easily.

1 Cut templates to the size of the finished shape. Pin to your choice of fabric. Cut out the shapes without seams and pin them to the main fabric.

2 To stab stitch around the edge of the appliqué, bring a threaded needle up through the fabric next to the appliqué. Take it back down, catching the edge of the appliqué.

Traditional appliqué

Choose simple shapes for appliqué because it is difficult to turn under raw edges on intricate shapes, and to keep lines smooth on tight curves. Cut motifs so that the grain matches the main fabric. Appliqué can be worked with or without an embroidery hoop. Sew the appliqué carefully to avoid fabric distortion.

1 Cut a template to the finished size and draw around it on the right side of the fabric. Cut out, adding a 5mm/¼in seam allowance all around.

2 Clip into the seam on inward-facing curves, and notch outward-facing curves. Cut up to the marked line, but not beyond it. Straight edges do not need clipping.

3 Pin the appliqué in place. Baste 1cm/½in in from the raw edge. Turn under the raw edge with the needle tip so that the pencil line disappears. Hem stitch along the fold.

Using freezer paper

Freezer paper is a wax-coated paper used to wrap food. The paper sticks firmly but temporarily to fabric if pressed with a medium iron. It is non-stain and can be peeled off easily.

1 Cut a template the exact size of the appliqué and draw around it on the dull side of the freezer paper. Cut out the shape along the lines.

2 Iron the shape to the wrong side of the fabric and cut out, adding a 5mm/¼in seam allowance all around.

Above: Strips and squares of brightly coloured fabric have been applied to a dark ground. The appliqué squares have been frayed and overstitched with freestyle machine embroidery.

3 Snip inward-facing curves close to the paper and make a notch in the seam of outward-facing curves. Turn under the raw edge and baste. Press again. The wax on the freezer paper will help the shape retain a crisp, neat edge.

4 Pin the shape in place on the main fabric and hem stitch in place. Use a small, fine needle and a thread (floss) in a colour to match the appliqué or background fabric.

5 Hem most of the way around the shape then remove the basting stitches. Slide your finger between the freezer paper and the appliqué and ease it out carefully. Hem the last section of the appliqué in place.

Machine embroidery

Whether your sewing machine is a wonder of modern technology or an old swing needle model, it will be suitable for machine embroidery. Technical advances have produced sewing machines that can stitch sophisticated computer-generated patterns, but machine embroidery is mainly worked using basic straight and zigzag stitches and is therefore well within the scope of most sewing machines.

Using the presser foot

There are two methods of working machine embroidery – with the presser foot in place on the machine; or using a darning foot instead of a presser foot, known as freestyle machine embroidery. Practise the different techniques on small pieces of fabric first and keep them in a notebook for future reference.

Movement is slightly restricted when working machine embroidery with the presser foot and with the feed teeth up, since the machine will allow you only to work backwards and forwards and not from side to side, but a variety of effects can be created using a basic straight stitch.

1 Thread the machine in the normal way with a synthetic sewing thread. Stitch in a straight line and stop with the needle in the fabric. Lift the presser foot and swing the fabric around ready to stitch the second row. Lower the presser foot and stitch again. Continue in this way until you have formed a block of straight lines.

2 With the needle still in the fabric, turn the embroidery around so that the next stitching lines you work will be horizontal. Stitch backwards and forwards across the previous stitching to create a cross-hatched pattern. Change the thread colour to build up layers of different-coloured lines.

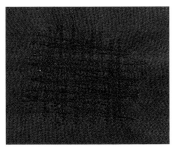

3 Straight stitches can be used to make parallel lines too. Sew across one or two stitches before beginning the next line. Stitch at right angles to form a regular grid pattern and fill in with diagonal lines to increase the texture and density of the stitches.

4 Altering the length of the stitches will produce different textures. Long stitches have a smooth appearance whereas small stitches tend to bring the bobbin thread up and make a slightly textured line. Use a different colour in the bobbin to emphasize this effect.

5 Heavier embroidery threads (floss), which cannot be threaded through the needle, can be wound on to the bobbin. Work with the fabric upside down and stitch in the normal way. The embroidery thread will then look as if it has been couched down.

Zigzag setting

Machine zigzag, or satin stitch, is commonly associated with appliqué, particularly fusible web appliqué, where the raw edge of the applied fabric is visible. Densely packed zigzag, worked over the raw edge, creates a neat outline.

1 Set the machine to a wide zigzag for machine embroidery. You may need to lengthen the stitch and loosen the tension slightly so that the stitches lie flat. Iron interfacing to the wrong side of the fabric before you start stitching if your fabric is delicate.

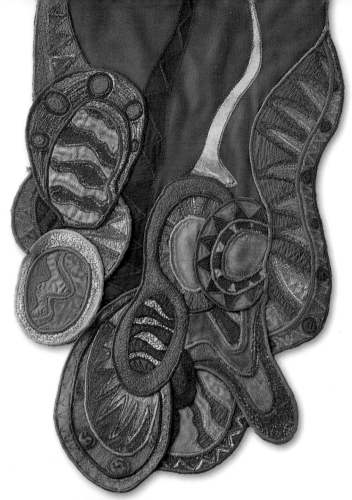

2 Work a row of zigzag stitches. Stop with the needle in the fabric. Turn the fabric around and stitch the next row.

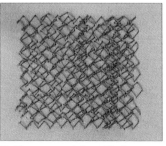

3 The rows can be worked slightly at an angle to produce a rough texture. Go back over some of the rows to increase the density of the stitches.

4 Work rows at right angles to the first set to make a denser cross-hatched pattern. Leave the needle in the fabric at the end of the row and swing the fabric around.

Top: Appliqué and satin stitch have been used to effect in this vibrantly coloured silk and satin scarf.

5 To create a regular grid of diamonds, work a row of zigzag stitches and stop with the needle in the fabric at the end of the left swing. Turn the fabric around and work the second row, guiding the fabric carefully to allow the needle to stitch into the points of the previous stitches. You will find it works better if you sew the rows quite quickly.

Using different feet

Most sewing machines have a selection of different feet which can be used for machine embroidery. An ordinary general-purpose foot is fine for basic straight or zigzag stitches, but you should change to a clear-view foot if you want to stitch along a curved line or in a precise direction.

Use an embroidery foot that is cut away underneath for working satin stitch, because this would be flattened by an ordinary foot. A cording foot has a groove underneath or a hole on top, to guide a cord or braid under the presser foot.

Using a cording foot

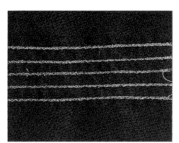

1 Place the braid on the fabric and put it under the cording foot. Make sure the braid is well under to ensure it does not bundle up under the foot. Work a couple of straight stitches in the end of the cord, then alter the stitch width to make a zigzag across the braid from one side to the other. Stitch slowly, letting the braid feed under the foot. Use the side of the foot as a guide when working multiple rows.

Machine-wrapped cords

Machine-wrapped cords are very attractive and quite easy to make. Use them as an added decoration on embroidery. You can make them using an ordinary foot and with the width set at its widest. Alternately, use a foot with a large groove or hole to let the cord go through easily, especially if the cord you are covering is thick. Any smooth, round cord is suitable, including lengths of wool (yarn).

1 Insert the cord through the hole in the foot and work one or two straight stitches to secure the threads.

2 Set the machine to its widest zigzag, and the stitch length at zero. Loosen the top tension slightly. Hold the cord on both sides of the cording foot and feed it through slowly as you stitch. Work over the cord again until it is completely covered.

Above: Machine-wrapped cords, appliqué, hand and freestyle machine embroidery on water-soluble fabric have been incorporated into this fan design.

Left: The basic wrapped cords.

Freestyle machine embroidery

This type of machine embroidery is worked with a darning foot, a special machine embroidery foot or a spring needle, and with the feed teeth lowered. The fabric lies flat against the needleplate, so that the stitch forms correctly. The fabric is also stretched taut in a hoop before beginning to stitch. With no restriction from the presser foot, movement becomes much more flexible and the stitching multi-directional.

Even if you are used to working with a sewing machine, this type of embroidery takes time to perfect. Think of it as drawing with pencil and paper, only here the paper (fabric) moves, rather than the pencil (needle).

Above: Freestyle machine embroidery is used here to define the design suggested by the painted background.

NEEDLES

Ordinary machine needles can be used for machine embroidery, although needles with larger eyes, which accommodate heavier threads, are available. Try size 90/14 to begin with and move on to size 80/12.

Hoops

Two types of hoop are suitable for freestyle machine embroidery. A traditional wooden hand embroidery hoop can be used, or one of the new flat metal and plastic spring hoops specially made for machine embroidery. These are designed to fit easily under the darning foot and to hold the fabric taut.

1 To use a wooden hoop, place the fabric right side up on top of the outer ring. Press the inner ring firmly in position. If the fabric slips, tighten the outer ring and re-fit the fabric.

2 Alternatively, place the fabric right side up on the plastic ring. Squeeze the handles of the ring together and press down into the plastic ring. Release the handles to secure the fabric.

Beginning freestyle machine embroidery

1 Insert a new needle size 90/14 in the machine. Loosen the tension slightly and fit the darning foot. Bring the thread up through the needle plate and lower the feed teeth.

2 Place the fabric and hoop under the foot. Hold the top thread and turn the hand wheel until the bobbin thread appears. Pull it through the fabric. Make the stitch length zero.

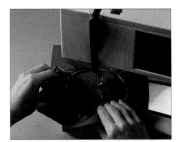

3 Lower the foot. This engages the stitch mechanism. Hold the thread ends and work a few stitches to secure the threads. Snip the thread ends if working an open pattern.

Vermicelli stitch

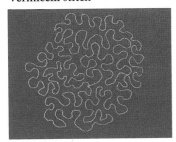

In vermicelli stitch the fabric is moved in all possible directions. This will help you learn to control the movement of the hoop and the speed of the machine. Work with the machine at a moderate speed and move the hoop to create a squiggly line, as shown. Try not to jerk the hoop as this could make the thread or needle snap.

Loose spirals

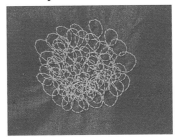

Spirals are formed by moving the hoop in a circular movement. Begin in the centre and work your way outwards. Stitch at moderate speed and move the hoop slowly and smoothly to make tight curves with lots of small stitches. The spirals can be formed outside or inside the line. It takes practice to make circles smooth, with even stitches.

Jagged spirals

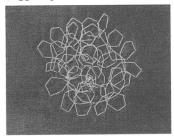

Jagged spirals are worked at a fast machine speed. Hold the hoop securely by the rim and secure the thread with a couple of straight stitches. Move the hoop in a circular movement as before. If you can get the speed of both the machine and the hoop right, jagged spirals will form. Try not to jerk suddenly or the needle will break.

Tight spirals

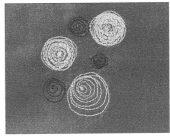

Tight spirals are slightly more difficult to work.

Bring the bobbin thread up to the surface and secure with a few stitches. Lift the darning foot and trim the thread neatly. Lower the darning foot and sew at a moderate speed, moving the hoop in a circular motion. Work slowly out from the centre and try to form a near-perfect circle. Spirals can be quite open or densely filled. If necessary, you can stitch back over the previous stitches to fill in between lines.

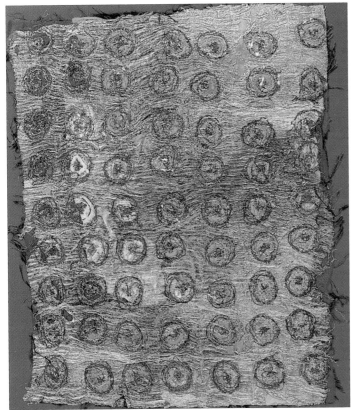

Left: This colourful design features machine-embroidered circles on multi-coloured metallic organza.

Creating different textures

Altering the tension of the machine changes the appearance of even a simple line of straight stitches. Tightening the top tension will bring the bobbin thread up to the surface and create a textured effect. You can emphasize this whipped effect by using a different colour in the reel and in the bobbin.

The top tension is always loosened slightly to begin freestyle machine stitching, so it makes quite a difference when the top tension is tightened completely. Take care that the top tension is not so tight that it causes the needle to bend and break.

If you want to create even more texture, loosen the lower tension by turning the screw on the bobbin case. If you are nervous about being able to get it back to the right setting again, try this tip. Before changing the lower tension, fit a bobbin in the case and let it dangle by the thread. You should be able to make the case drop bit by bit by jerking the thread lightly. This is the correct lower tension.

Whipping

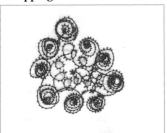

Tighten the top tension and work whipped loops and spirals. You can alter the tonal appearance by changing the speed of stitching. If you stitch slowly, the top thread will sometimes be couched by the bobbin thread. Increase the speed and the stitches get smaller and the bobbin thread covers more of the top thread.

Whipping with loops

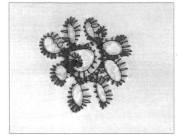

Bring the top tension back slightly and loosen the lower tension. Move the hoop quickly to pull the bobbin thread out and make quite distinct loops. As the spiral size increases, the loops are pulled out further. Experiment to create different effects by changing the colour and texture of the bobbin thread.

Loop texture

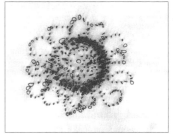

A different texture is created if the top thread is pulled out completely. Cut the top thread between the loops every so often and pull it out carefully. Use this technique for landscape backgrounds or filling large surface areas.

Whipped spots

If the lower tension is loosened considerably and the top tension tightened enough, much longer loops will form. Use this setting to make very textured whorls or little spots. Leave the thread ends until last, then sew them through to the wrong side.

Whipping on muslin

The fabric you use will affect the final appearance of the stitch, too. If you work whipping on a loosely woven muslin, the fabric threads will be pulled and distorted too.

Gathering on felt

Tighten the top tension and fit the felt under the darning foot (this will be the wrong side). Move the felt in a circular movement to stitch fairly big spirals and loops. The tight top thread will cause the fabric to gather. Do not use an embroidery hoop.

Zigzag and satin stitch

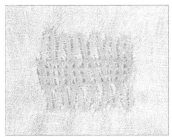

1 Set the machine for the widest stitch and loosen the top tension slightly so that only the top thread shows in the stitched sample. Work up and down, varying the speed of the machine in relation to the movement of the hoop to produce lines of zigzag and satin stitching.

2 Wider areas of satin stitching can be built up by overlapping adjacent rows. Or the width of the stitch can be changed as you work to produce thick and thin lines. Move the hoop with one hand and turn the stitch width dial with the other. Try to make the transition even.

3 When you work satin stitch on a loose-weave fabric such as muslin you can create machine embroidery that looks like traditional drawn-thread work. The swing of the needle pulls the fabric threads together to produce a lacy effect.

The background fabric

Machine stitching looks quite different on different types of fabrics. For example, a design stitched on a smooth fabric has a smooth finish compared to one stitched on velvet or a pile fabric, where the stitches seem to sink into the background.

The background does to some extent affect the type of embroidery you choose. On transparent fabrics, such as muslin, the threads can be seen from the wrong side of the fabric and the stitches tend to pull the fabric and create small holes. Satin stitching on loose-weave fabrics such as scrim pulls the threads together to produce an extremely lacy effect. Straight stitching works better on net, where there is considerable contrast between the stitching and the background.

Below: Machine embroidery on bubble wrap, a non-traditional fabric, creates a most unusual effect.

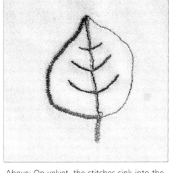

Above: On velvet, the stitches sink into the pile to give a very soft effect.

Above: On net, the stitching is very prominent. Take care not to tear the fabric when machine stitching.

Using water-soluble fabric

Water-soluble fabric allows you to create three-dimensional pieces of embroidery that can be attached to another background, or used to create sculptured pieces. The soluble material, which looks like clear film (plastic wrap), is fitted in a hoop and machine embroidered as if it were fabric. Even if you intend to work zigzag stitches, use straight stitch initially because the zigzag stitches will unravel if worked on their own.

The material is dissolved in water, leaving the embroidery behind.

There are two types available: a thin clear plastic sheet that dissolves in cold water, and a pale green muslin that is soluble in hot water.

Open circles
Care must be taken when working open work on water-soluble fabric. Check that all parts of the embroidery outline are joined so that the stitched piece does not fall apart in the water. Hold the embroidery up to the light to check for gaps. If necessary, go back over some lines to close gaps.

1 Stretch the soluble material in the hoop. Slip the hoop under the darning foot and bring the bobbin thread up through the soluble material as you would for normal machine embroidery.

2 Set the machine for straight stitch with the stitch length almost at zero. Lower the darning foot and work a few stitches to secure the thread. Trim the ends. Begin to move the hoop in small circular movements.

3 Ensure that the circles touch one another, interlocking all over the material. Overstitch the circles several times and with different colours, if appropriate. The denser the stitching, the stronger the piece will be.

Filled shapes
Flowers and other solid shapes can be created with a solid filling stitch. The soluble plastic will tear quite easily so a piece of net can be fitted into the hoop at the same time for added strength. Pieces of fabric or thread can also be sandwiched between the two layers before stitching.

1 Mark the shape to be stitched with a water-soluble ink pen.

2 Outline the shape with rows of stitching, then fill in the shape.

Dissolving the soluble fabric
Fill a shallow dish with water and place the embroidered piece in it. Agitate the embroidery between your fingers until the material dissolves away. Rinse and leave to dry flat. You can pin very fine pieces to polystyrene (styrofoam), so that the shape does not distort when it is in the water.

Above: Shapes stitched on water-soluble fabric have been applied to the lid of this small beaded purse.

The sewing machine

A sewing machine is one of the most expensive pieces of sewing equipment you will buy and you should take as much care choosing one as you would a washing machine or a car. Think about how much sewing you expect to do, not only next year but also ten or twenty years ahead.

Types of machine

All sewing machines sew a line of simple straight stitches, but new technology means there are many different types on the market.

Basic straight stitch and zigzag
The only basic straight stitch machines around today are antiques – but they still form beautiful stitches. Zigzag stitches move the needle from side to side. The stitch width and spacing can be altered.

Automatic
Automatic machines can move the fabric backwards and forwards while stitching to produce stretch stitches, saddle stitch and overlocking. They have special discs inside called pattern cams that produce a variety of elaborate embroidery stitches.

Electronic
Electronic machines (above) are smoother and more sophisticated than ordinary automatic machines. The motor is controlled electronically and stops as soon as you lift your foot from the pedal. The machine can also sew very slowly if required with the same power. Electronic machines can be automatic or computerized, having either cams or a computer to create the stitches.

Computerized
Computerized machines (above) are advanced models with silicon chips instead of pattern cams and are capable of a huge range of ornamental stitches. The stitches can be more complicated because the fabric can move in all directions. Touch-button panels or screens make them simple to use and some can stitch small motifs, or even your own designs when linked to a personal computer.

CHOOSING A SEWING MACHINE

Most people only ever use the straight stitch and zigzag on a sewing machine so think carefully before spending a lot of money on technology you don't really need. If you intend to make soft furnishings and curtains, a sturdy, secondhand flatbed machine may be best. Free-arm machines have a narrow arm that extends above the base to allow fabric to be moved around and are more suitable for dressmaking.

Take samples of different fabrics such as jersey, silk and denim with you and try them out folded double on the machines. Check that threading up is easy and the bobbin case is not difficult to handle. Check that the electric fittings and attachments are well made.

Find out what accessories are included and if parts are easily replaced. Finally check that the machine packs away easily and isn't too heavy. After all, they're supposed to be portable.

Spend some time reading the manual and becoming familiar with the different parts. If you haven't used a sewing machine before, practise sewing on paper without thread first. For this, set all the dials at zero except for the stitch length, which should be between 2 and 3. Using lined paper, go up and down the lines, then try stopping and reversing, and very slowly, following curves and circles. Once you are comfortable, practise the same techniques on a double layer of gingham fabric.

Know your machine

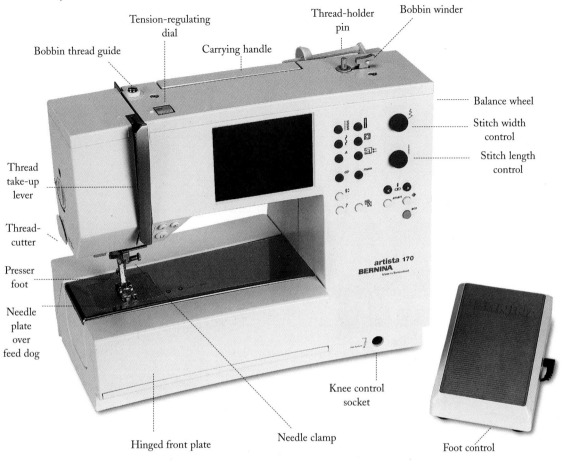

Tension-regulating dial

Bobbin thread guide

Carrying handle

Thread-holder pin

Bobbin winder

Balance wheel

Stitch width control

Stitch length control

Thread take-up lever

Thread-cutter

Presser foot

Needle plate over feed dog

artista 170
BERNINA

Knee control socket

Hinged front plate

Needle clamp

Foot control

Balance wheel
This controls the sewing machine. On manual machines, turn the wheel to lower the needle.

Bobbin winder
This allows you to fill the bobbin quickly and evenly.

Foot control/knee contol
This starts, stops and controls the speed that the machine stitches.

Needle clamp
This secures the shaft of the needle into the machine.

Needle plate
The needle plate surrounds the feed teeth and has a hole for the needle.

Presser foot
This holds the fabric flat on the needle plate so that a stitch can form.

Stitch length control
Use this to alter the length of straight stitch and the density of zigzag stitch.

Stitch width control
This controls the amount the needle moves sideways. Use a suitable presser foot so that the needle doesn't break.

Thread take-up lever
This feeds the correct amount of thread from the spool down through to the needle.

Tension-regulating dial
The tension dial alters the tension on the top thread.

Thread-cutter
This is situated at the back of the machine for cutting threads.

Thread-holder pin
This holds the reel of thread when filling the bobbin and stitching.

Threading the upper machine

Unless a machine is threaded in exactly the right sequence it won't work properly. Every machine has a slightly different sequence, but in all of them the thread goes between the tension discs and back up through the take-up lever before it is threaded through the needle.

Always have the take-up lever at its highest point before threading. This brings the needle up to its highest point and lines up all the mechanical parts inside the sewing machine ready for inserting the filled bobbin case. The manual accompanying your sewing machine should have a diagram showing the correct threading sequence for your particular model.

Horizontal thread-holders on the upper machine have a clip to hold the reel in position. The thread unwinds off one end of the stationary reel. Vertical thread-holders have a disc of felt to help the reel to spin around as the machine is working.

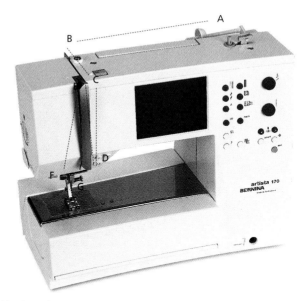

1 Fit the reel on to the thread-holder (A), making sure that the thread can come off freely. Take the thread round B, between the tension disks (C) and down under the first thread guide (D).

2 Put the thread into the top of the take-up lever (E) and then through the thread guides (F) leading down to the needle (G). Thread the needle from the grooved side (front to back).

Filling the bobbin

1 Fill the bobbin using the bobbin-winding mechanism on the machine. To begin, pass the end of the thread through one of the small holes in the side and fit it on to the spindle.

2 Click the bobbin-winding mechanism into place. This should automatically stop the machine from stitching – if not, you will have to loosen the stop motion knob on the hand wheel. The bobbin will fill automatically to the correct level.

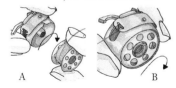

A   B

3 Insert the bobbin into the bobbin case (A) so that the thread is pulled back on itself through the spring (B).

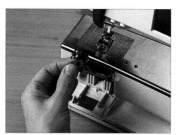

4 Fit the bobbin case into the machine, holding the case by the lever on the back. The open lever locks the bobbin into the case.

5 Push the case into the socket until it clicks then release the lever. Close the cover. If it does not click, the mechanism inside is not aligned.

The bobbin thread

1 To raise the bobbin thread, thread the needle and hold the upper thread out to one side. Some machines have an automatic thread-lifting mechanism but otherwise turn the hand wheel forwards until the needle has gone down and up again. Pull the upper thread to bring the bobbin thread right out. Take both threads through the slot in the presser foot and out of the back.

Choosing a needle

Always select a machine needle to
suit the thread and fabric you are
using; this will reduce the likelihood
of the needle breaking.

1 Universal needles
Universal sewing machine needles
range in size from 70/9, used for fine
fabrics, to 110/18, used for heavy-
weight fabrics. Size 80/12 is ideal
for medium-weight fabric. Keep a
selection to hand and change your
needle when using different weights
of fabric. A fine needle will break if
the fabric is too thick and a large
needle will damage a fine fabric.

2 Ballpoint needles
Ballpoint needles are used for
synthetic fabrics, jersey and elastic.
They have a round end which pushes
between the threads instead of
piercing them. This type of needle
can also be used with fine silks and
delicate fabrics which may snag.

3 Twin needles
Twin needles consist of two needles
fitted to the one shank. They are used
to sew narrow, parallel lines or, when
the machine tension is altered, to sew
pin tucks. You can also buy special
stretch twin needles for working on
jersey fabrics. When threading the
machine with these needles, you will
need two reels of thread. For best
results, take one thread down each
side of the central tension disc.

4 Wing needles
Wing needles have a wide blade on
each side of the shaft, which cuts a
decorative groove in the fabric as
you stitch.

5 Spring needles
A spring needle allows you to
embroider without a darning foot
or embroidery hoop because it stops
the fabric from moving about.

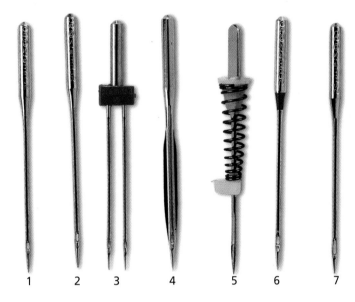

1   2   3   4   5   6   7

6 Embroidery needles
Embroidery needles have larger eyes
than normal to allow sewing with a
wide range of decorative threads
(floss). Some special embroidery
needles have extremely large eyes for
the thicker threads.

7 Top-stitch needles
Top-stitch needles have a very
large eye to accommodate a thick,
decorative thread.

FITTING THE NEEDLE

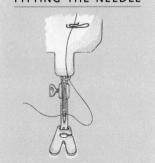

Machine needles can only be
fitted one way because they
have a flat surface down one side
(the shank) and a long groove
down the other side (the shaft).
When the needle is inserted, this
groove should line up directly
with the last thread guide. When
the machine is in use, the thread
runs down the groove and scores
a unique channel into the metal.
So when you change the type of
thread, you should change your
needle, too.

Machine feet

All machines have a number of interchangeable feet for different types of sewing. The most common ones are illustrated here but you can buy other specialist feet. These are designed for particular functions such as getting close to a zipper or guiding thread, cord or fabric while sewing.

Clear-view foot

Similar to the general-purpose foot, this foot allows you to see where you are stitching. It can be cut away or made from clear plastic. It can also be used for satin stitch because the underside of the foot is cut away to prevent the stitching from being flattened. Use it when working with bulky fabrics.

Hemming foot

A hemming foot has a curled piece of metal that turns a rolled hem on fine fabrics and feeds it under the needle. The hem can then be stitched with straight or fancy stitches.

Cording foot

This foot has a groove underneath which guides cord, round elastic or narrow ribbon under the needle for stitching.

Blind-hemming (blind-stitching) foot

This foot has a metal guide for a turned-back hem. It is possible to adjust the needle position so that just a few threads are caught when stitching.

General-purpose foot

The basic metal general-purpose foot shown is used for all general straight stitching and zigzag on ordinary fabrics.

Darning foot

A darning foot is used for machine darning and freestyle machine embroidery. The feed teeth on the machine are always lowered and the fabric is held flat against the needle plate, using an embroidery hoop upside down. Set the stitch length at zero and sew straight stitch or zigzag with this foot.

Zipper foot

This allows you to stitch close to zipper teeth or piping. The needle can be adjusted to sew on either side. A special zipper foot is available to guide the teeth of invisible zippers.

Buttonhole foot

This foot has two grooves underneath to guide rows of satin stitch forwards and backwards, leaving a tiny gap between for cutting.

Spacing guide (seam guide)

This attachment can be used with a variety of different feet as long as the rod and clip fits. By sliding the rod along, a particular distance can be stitched accurately. This guide is useful for stitching curves and for machine quilting.

Stitch tension

A new machine will have the tension correctly set, with the dial at the marked centre point. Try out any stitches you intend to use on a sample of your fabric.

To check the tension, bring all the pattern and zigzag dials back to zero and set the stitch length between 2 and 3 for normal stitching. Place a folded strip of fabric on the needle plate, lower the needle into the fabric and sew a row of straight stitches. These should look exactly the same on both sides.

Above: The top and bottom threads lock together correctly in the middle of the fabric when the machine tension is correct.

Above: The top tension is loose and it is pulled to the wrong side of the fabric.

Above: The top thread tension is too tight.

Altering tension

To tighten the tension, turn the dial towards the lower numbers. To loosen it, turn towards the higher numbers. This will automatically affect the tension of the thread coming through the bobbin case. If the top tension dial is far from the centre, the spring on the bobbin case is probably wrong.

Only alter the lower tension as a last resort. You should be able to dangle the bobbin case without the thread slipping through. Shake the thread and the bobbin case should drop a little. Turn the screw on the side of the bobbin case slightly to alter the tension. Try out the stitching again on a sample of fabric and alter the top tension this time until the stitch is perfect.

Maintenance and trouble-shooting

Like a car, a sewing machine will only run well if it is used regularly and looked after. It needs to be oiled on a regular basis and cleaned out – this may be several times during the making of curtains or a garment. General maintenance only takes a few minutes but will ensure that your machine works well and lasts longer between services. Cleaning is essential when you change fabrics, especially if it is from a dark to a light-coloured one. Remove the sewing machine needle. Use a stiff brush to clean out the fluff (lint) along the route the top thread takes through the machine. Unscrew the needle plate and brush out any fluff from around the feed teeth. Remove the bobbin case to check that no thread is trapped in the mechanism.

Oil the machine from time to time using your handbook as a guide. Only use a couple of drops – too much oil can be damaging. Leave the machine overnight with a fabric pad beneath the presser foot and then wipe the needle before use. Some new machines are self-lubricating.

Even if you take care of your machine, problems can occur. Some of the more common problems are listed below.

The machine works too slowly

The machine may have two speeds and may be set on slow. More likely, it hasn't been used for a while and oil could be clogging the working parts. Run the machine without a needle for a minute to loosen all the joints. Check that the foot control is not obstructed. As a last resort, ask a dealer to check the tension belt.

No stitches form

Ensure the bobbin is full and inserted correctly. Check that the needle is facing in the right direction and threaded from the grooved side.

Above: Lace and velvet require extreme care when sewing. Always test a sample first to establish the correct tension.

The needle doesn't move

Check that the balance wheel is tight and that the bobbin winder is switched off. If the needle still doesn't move there may be thread trapped in the sewing hook behind the bobbin case. Remove the bobbin case and take hold of the thread end. Rock the balance wheel backwards and forwards until it comes out.

The machine jams

Rock the balance wheel gently to loosen the threads and take the fabric out. Remove the needle, unscrew the needle plate and brush out any fluff. Alternatively check that the machine is correctly threaded and the fabric is far enough under the presser foot when beginning.

The needle bends or breaks

A needle will break if it hits the foot, bobbin case or needle plate on a machine. Check that you are using the correct foot. When using a zipper foot, a common mistake is forgetting to move the needle to the left or right for straight stitching or zigzag. Check the bobbin case is inserted properly. Make sure the take-up lever is at its highest point before fitting.

A needle that has been bent will break if it hits the needle plate. To avoid bent needles, sew slowly over

pins and thick seams. A needle will also bend if there is a knot in the thread or if the fabric is pulled through the machine faster than the machine is sewing.

Fabric does not feed through

This can happen when the feed teeth are lowered in the darning position. Close zigzag or embroidery stitches will bunch up in the general-purpose foot, so change the foot to one that is cut away underneath to allow the stitches to feed through.

The stitches are different lengths

Check whether the needle is blunt or unsuitable for the fabric and that it is inserted correctly. Try stitching with the needle in the left and right position. On fine fabrics, put tissue paper under the presser foot.

The top thread keeps breaking

Manufacturers recommend that you change needles every time you change the type of thread. This is because each thread type scores a unique channel through the needle groove which will cause a different type of thread to snag and break. Label your needle packet to indicate what type of thread to use with each needle. This is particularly important when doing machine embroidery. Check that you are using the correct thread and type of needle for the fabric. A knot or slub in the thread may also cause the thread to break.

The bobbin thread breaks

Check that the bobbin case is inserted correctly, has not been overfilled and the thread has no knots in it. Also check the bobbin case mechanism for trapped fluff. Occasionally, the spring on the bobbin case is too tight for the thread and the tension screw has to be loosened – refer to your user manual for instructions.

INDEX

Templates

Blackwork, p.58

Mountmellick, p.68

SUPPLIERS

United Kingdom
Barnyarns Ltd
PO Box 28
Thirsk
North Yorkshire, YO7 3YN
for sewing and embroidery supplies

Bogod Machine Company
50–52 Great Sutton Street
London, EC1V ODJ
for sewing machines and overlockers

Coats Crafts
McMullen Road
Darlington
Co. Durham, DL1 1YQ
*for machine embroidery and
sewing threads*

Delicate Stitches
339 Kentish Town Road
Kentish Town
London
NW5 2TJ
for fine natural fabrics

DMC Creative World
Pullman Road
Wigston
Leicestershire, LE18 2DY
*for counted-thread fabrics, embroi-
dery thread and crewel wool*

House of Smocking
1 Ryeworth Road
Charlton Kings
Cheltenham,
Gloucestershire, GL52 6LG
for all smocking supplies

Newey Goodman
Sedgley Road
West Tipton
West Midlands
DY4 8AH
for sewing equipment

Ribbon Designs
PO Box 382
Edgware
Middlesex
HA8 7XQ
for silk ribbons

United States
Aardvark Adventures
PO Box 2449
Livermore, CA94551
for fabrics, threads and trims

Herrschers
Hoover Road
Stevens Point, WI 54481
for general tools and equipment

Nancy's Notions
PO Box 683
Dept 32, Beave Dam
WI 53916
*for sewing, quilting, beadwork,
appliqué and embroidery*

Australia
Coats Patons Crafts Pty Ltd
89–91 Peters Avenue
Mulgrave
VIC 3170

DMC Needlecraft Pty Ltd
51–55 Carrington Road
Marrickville
NSW 2204

Simply Stitches
153 Victoria Avenue
Chatswood
NSW 2067

Canada
Dressew
337 W Hastings Street
Vancouver, BC

ACKNOWLEDGEMENTS

The publisher would like to thank the talented stitchers who generously loaned their treasured embroideries and patchwork quilts
for inclusion in this publication: Daphne J Ashby, p.57 and p.74; Gilda Baron, p.10; Marilyn Becker, p.43 centre; Samantha Bourne, p.35;
Corynna Bridgwood for the canvas work cushion on p.7; Rosalind Brook Ross, p.27 and p.33; Kay Dennis, p.69; Diana Dolman, p.76;
Greta Fitchett, p.79; Peggy Field, p.83; Joy Frey, p.81; Jane Hopkins, p.82; Heide Jenkins, p.61; Denise Jones, p.47; Ann Mockford, p.77;
Jane Rodgers, p.87; Samiah Faridi Saeed, p.84 and p.86; and Angela Thompson, p.62.

Many thanks to the following people for stitching the many samples that appear in this publication: Sue Copeman, Barbara Lethbridge,
Joyce Mallinson, Brenda Monk, Kath Poxon, Suraiya Kidia Reed, Lynn Simms, Barbara Smith, Adele and Hayley Wainwright, and Rita Whitehorn.

Thanks also to the Bogod Machine Company for the loan of the sewing machine.

Thank you to the following for granting permission to reproduce images:
p.20, p.41 V&A Picture Library.